Published by Avocet Books
www.avocetbooks.com

Copyright © 2026 Marianne Lehikoinen
All rights reserved. This book or parts thereof may not be reproduced in any form, stored in any retrieval system, or transmitted in any form by any means—electronic, mechanical, photocopy, recording, or otherwise—without prior written permission of the author, except as provided by United States of America copyright law.

ISBNs:
eBook   978-1-963678-24-6
Paperback   978-1-963678-22-2
Hardcover   978-1-963678-23-9

First Edition

By reading this document, the reader agrees that under no circumstances is the author or the publisher responsible for any losses, direct or indirect, which are incurred as a result of the use of information contained within this document, including, but not limited to, errors, omissions, or inaccuracies.

BREAK THROUGH

FROM SOLO HUSTLE TO SCALABLE SUCCESS

MARIANNE LEHIKOINEN

To my husband and daughters.

CONTENTS

INTRODUCTION		1
CHAPTER 1.	BELIEVE BEFORE YOU SEE IT	7
CHAPTER 2.	THE FIRST BIG BREAKTHROUGH	21
CHAPTER 3.	PRODUCT AND CLIENT FULFILLMENT—DELIVERING RESULTS AT SCALE	37
CHAPTER 4.	THE SOLOPRENEUR TRAP AND THE PAIN OF SCALING	61
CHAPTER 5.	LEADERSHIP—FROM DOER TO LEADER	85
CHAPTER 6.	MARKETING—GROWING AN AUDIENCE AND GENERATING LEADS	103
CHAPTER 7.	SALES—SELLING WITH CONFIDENCE AND SYSTEMIZING GROWTH	127
CHAPTER 8.	PERSONAL BRANDING AND PR—BECOMING THE AUTHORITY	143
CHAPTER 9.	SUSTAINABLE SUCCESS—BUILDING A BUSINESS THAT SCALES FOR YOU	167
CHAPTER 10.	DESIGNING A LIFE YOU DON'T NEED TO ESCAPE FROM	191
CONCLUSION		207
ACKNOWLEDGMENTS		211
ABOUT THE AUTHOR		213

INTRODUCTION

"What does success mean to you?"
     I was young when I asked my mother that question—too young to fully understand what success was, but old enough to know I wanted it. Her answer has stayed with me all these years:

"Everyone wants that…but no one ever gets it."

Even as a child, that didn't sit right with me. I could see that some people *did* achieve success—so why not me? This moment planted a quiet defiance in me. A belief that if I wanted more, if I worked for it and figured out how to do it differently, I could build a life on my own terms.

Back then, no one in my family was talking about entrepreneurship or vision boards. I didn't have models for big dreams. My mom raised me and my sister alone, and our world was filled with practical, steady careers—nurses, teachers, engineers. Everyone worked hard and pretty much stayed in their lane.

I didn't want to stay in any old lane, however. I wanted to *create my own* lane.

I didn't have a clear picture of what that would look like, but I knew I was willing to try things other people wouldn't. Whether it was starting a blog at fifteen, recording my voice and sending demos to record labels, or putting my ideas out into the world before I felt ready, I wasn't afraid to take risks.

What I began to realize over time is that ambition isn't something to hide or apologize for—it's something to embrace and channel. And there were other women out there just like me. Women who were smart, capable, and full of potential. They weren't waiting for permission. They wanted to create their own lanes too.

Years later, I built my company to serve those women. Women like you. Women who are hungry for growth but overwhelmed by how to achieve it.

And that's why I wrote this book.

Why You're Here

If you picked up this book, chances are you're looking for a *breakthrough*.

Maybe you're tired of running your business alone—stretched too thin, trying to keep up with client work, sales calls, marketing, and the endless to-do list that never seems to shrink. You've built something you care about, but it's starting to feel like it's running you instead of the other way around.

Or maybe you've already had some success. You've reached a level of stability, but you can't shake the feeling that you're stuck. You see other entrepreneurs scaling with ease, charging more, building teams, and stepping fully into leadership roles. You know you're capable of that too—you just don't know what to do next.

Maybe you feel like there's a ceiling you can't quite break through. You're ready to grow, but you don't have the systems, the support, or the strategy to get there.

This book will help you bridge the gap between where you are today and where you want to be. It will give you the roadmap to transition from being the person who *does everything* to the leader of a sustainable, scalable business that works without you being in every detail.

Here's what you'll discover inside these pages:

- How to believe in your vision even when the numbers haven't caught up yet
- Why doing everything yourself is a trap and how to step into true leadership
- The strategy behind simplifying your offer so it actually scales
- How to grow your audience and generate leads without chasing trends or burning out on social media
- Why sales is service and how to sell with confidence and heart
- How to deliver results at scale so clients succeed without you working 24/7
- What sustainable scaling actually looks like (and why rushing growth creates chaos)

- How to design a business that supports your lifestyle instead of one that takes it over

Each chapter blends story, mindset, and strategy. You'll also see my journey—the good, the bad, and the messy middle. You'll meet clients and case studies that prove you're not alone in these challenges. And most importantly, you'll gain practical tools you can use right away to create momentum in your own business.

This book isn't about theory. It's about real-world steps that you can implement as you read. By the end, you'll not only know what to do—you'll understand how to think differently, make decisions like a CEO, and build a business that truly works.

Why I Can Help You Build What You Want

I started my business with a simple mission: to help women be shamelessly ambitious and boldly pursue their goals. From the very beginning, it was never just about making money; I wanted to create something meaningful—something that would give women the tools, confidence, and support to stop doing everything alone and finally build the businesses (and life) they dreamed of.

Like many of you, I didn't come from a background where entrepreneurship was the norm. I was born and raised in a small town in Northern Finland, by a single mother. In our world, success meant stability, not risk-taking. No one in my family was talking about building a company, hiring a team, or creating wealth. There were no models for this kind of life.

When I started, I had no audience, no connections, and no capital. All I had was a vision and a willingness to act on it. I made every mistake you can imagine. I took on too much, worked around the clock, and tried to do everything myself.

But through trial and error, I built something extraordinary.

I founded Smart Mentoring in 2020, and in less than two and a half years, we grew from zero to consistent six figures in monthly revenue. That chapter in my journey was shared widely in Finland, but behind the headlines were countless long days, hard lessons, and a team learning as we went.

Today, we help skilled coaches, consultants, and service-based founders turn their expertise into high-revenue, system-driven businesses—without burning out, trading time for money, or losing themselves in the process.

None of my success happened by chance. Over the years, I've invested hundreds of thousands of dollars in mentors, coaches, and masterminds so I could learn how to run and scale a business efficiently. And just as importantly, I've spent the last six years solving these challenges every working day—in my own company and inside the businesses of our clients.

That's why our work is so effective: It was built in the trenches, not in theory.

At the time of writing this, we've now served nearly 600 experts, coaches, and consultants, helping them raise their prices with confidence, build teams that truly support them, and create consistent $20,000 to $80,000 months—often organically, without complicated funnels or gimmicks.

In 2024, I was honored to be named Young Entrepreneur of the Year in Espoo, Finland. My first book, *Sivubisnes* (Otava, 2021), became one of the first mainstream Finnish books to shine a spotlight on side hustles and helped spark a new generation of Nordic entrepreneurs.

But behind every milestone is a bigger mission: to help one million women become too wealthy to be silenced so they can own their power, speak their truth, and change the world. My long-term vision is to become one of the most influential business voices of my generation and to reshape what leadership looks like on a global stage.

I share this not to impress you, but to show you what's possible. My journey from outsider to industry leader is living proof that you can create opportunity from nothing—and that with the right strategies, systems, and mindset shifts, you can scale a business that changes not only your life, but also the lives of those you lead and serve.

This book is my way of helping you do exactly that.

What This Book Is and Isn't

This book is for solo entrepreneurs—especially women who've built businesses around their expertise, whether through coaching, consulting, courses, or digital products—and who are ready to *breakthrough* to the next level.

It's for those who want to scale without losing their personal touch. Who want to grow a business that's profitable and sustainable without running themselves into the ground.

This book isn't about building a massive company to sell or acquire. It's not about chasing every new trend or social media hack, hoping for a quick win either. And it's definitely not about hustling harder or working 100-hour weeks to get ahead. If you're looking for quick fixes or overnight success stories, you won't find them here.

Instead, this book is a roadmap to help you transition from solopreneur to entrepreneur by building systems and leading a small but mighty team. It's a framework for creating freedom and impact without losing the heart and soul of your business. Most importantly, it's a collection of proven strategies you can adapt to your unique goals and vision, so you can grow in a way that feels sustainable.

This book exists because there's a gap in the market for women like you—women who aren't just chasing revenue for revenue's sake, but who also want more control over their time, more confidence in their leadership, and more consistency between their business and their life.

Why *Breakthrough*

The word *breakthrough* gets used a lot in business, but here, it means something deeper. A breakthrough isn't just a big win or a lucky moment. It's a shift: a clear line between how things were and how they will be going forward.

For some entrepreneurs, a breakthrough comes when they finally realize their business has the potential to scale. After months or even years of feeling stuck, they see a path forward that doesn't require them to personally do everything.

For others, it's a decision. The moment they finally raise their prices and stop underselling themselves. The moment they claim their authority and step into the role of CEO instead of staying stuck as just the service provider.

It can also be a sense of relief—the day you watch your team handle things beautifully without you needing to step in or hover. That's when you see proof that the systems you've built actually work, and you can finally let go of some of the weight you've been carrying.

But breakthroughs aren't just external. They can also be deeply *personal*. They happen when you confront old patterns and beliefs that have held you back. Maybe you've been taught to play small, to avoid making waves, or to tie your worth to how hard you work. Breaking through those limitations isn't easy, but it is essential. Because while scaling a business is about strategy, it's also about becoming the kind of leader who can handle what comes next.

This book is about helping you create those breakthroughs—step by step, layer by layer. Some will happen quickly, like landing a high-ticket client or setting a boundary that frees up hours of your time. Others will take longer, like reshaping how you think about money, leadership, or what's possible for you.

By the time you finish this book, you'll have the tools, strategies, and mindset shifts to not just dream about that next level, but to make it real.

You've already built something amazing. Now, it's time to take it further—to step into the role you've been preparing for and build the business you've always known was possible.

Let's get to work.

CHAPTER 1
BELIEVE BEFORE YOU SEE IT

"You could build a million-dollar business."

My mentor said it like a weather report—calm, certain, ordinary. To me, it felt outrageous. At the time I was stitching together tiny wins, juggling side projects, and trying to believe that any of it would add up.

A million dollars wasn't on my horizon. Saving for a house down payment was.

But that sentence lodged itself in my mind. I couldn't prove it. I couldn't model it in a spreadsheet. I could only choose to believe it long before there was evidence. That was the first real act of entrepreneurship for me. It wasn't a launch or a funnel, but a decision: to hold a bigger vision than my current results.

This chapter is about that decision. The season when belief has to run ahead of proof. When you're still building in the dark, betting on a future no one else can see yet. If you're standing there now—tired, hopeful, unproven—consider this your permission slip. The breakthrough rarely arrives on schedule. But it does meet the person who believes as if it's already on the way.

A Mission Takes Shape

Back in 2019, I launched a company called Career Girl.

Career Girl began as a simple Facebook group—a safe space for ambitious women like me who were often told we were "*too much.*" Too loud. Too driven. Too ambitious. I wanted to create a community where that drive didn't need to be explained or apologized for, a place where women could show up fully as themselves.

When I launched the group, I had no idea if anyone would join. To my absolute delight, however, by the end of the very first weekend, a hundred women had signed up. As part of the group intake, I had asked a single question: "What do you need help with?" Over and over again, women wrote the same thing: "I want to turn my passion into a business."

That one phrase became the heartbeat of everything I would build. It shaped my first offer, gave me clarity on my message, and ultimately became my mission. Even at the start of my pregnancy—when things felt uncertain and I wasn't sure if I should, or even could, commit to building a business—I held onto that vision. When my health steadied and the path cleared, I went all in. I pushed through exhaustion, nausea, and endless doctor visits to launch my first course and serve that group. It wasn't just about teaching women how to sell. It was about helping them claim futures they'd been told weren't possible—futures built around their passions and purpose rather than someone else's expectations. That mission lit a fire in me, one that burned bright even when everything else felt uncertain.

But passion alone wasn't enough to pay the bills.

From the outside, it looked like Career Girl was gaining traction. The Facebook group kept growing, our audience was engaged, and a few course launches even looked successful on the surface. But behind the scenes, it was a different story.

I was hustling nonstop—hosting free webinars, recording podcasts, creating endless content, testing out new offers, doing paid collaborations on social media, launching mini-workshops. I was constantly chasing the next idea, hoping *this* would be the thing that finally worked. Some days, I'd be working from early morning until midnight, tinkering with Canva graphics, writing copy, replying to every single DM, and answering every group question personally.

It wasn't just long hours—it was mental overload. There was no plan, no strategy, just me throwing spaghetti at the wall and hoping something stuck.

Each launch gave me a brief surge of revenue, a momentary high that faded as quickly as it came. Then there would be weeks of silence, bills piling up, and me wondering how to keep the lights on. Every dollar

I earned went straight back into the business—mentorship, ads, the agency running them, online courses, software. By the end of that first year, I was a few thousand dollars in the red, still pouring everything in and wondering when it would finally be enough.

By the summer of 2021, the company was stretched so thin that I was $7,300 in the red. My husband and I were forced to sell our car. We paused our mortgage payments. My husband had returned to school, and part of his student loan was being used to keep my business alive. I felt like I was holding my dream together with duct tape, scrambling to keep everything from collapsing.

There were nights I lay awake, staring at the ceiling, completely drained. My body ached from the constant stress, my mind was foggy, and my spirit felt crushed under the weight of it all. I wasn't thinking about finding a safer job—I knew I could always go back to freelancing or start another side hustle if I needed to because I'd done it before. My first business, launched in 2017, had supported me through my studies and after graduation. But this time was different. I wasn't just trying to employ myself; I was trying to build something bigger, something that could also create opportunities for others.

That's what made the waiting so hard. I was impatient for momentum, desperate for proof that all the effort and sacrifice would finally amount to something. And yet, no matter how hopeless it seemed, I couldn't quit. Because deep down, I wasn't just building a business—I was chasing my vision. A vision for the women who had joined that group and dared to believe they could have more. And a vision for my own family and the future I wanted to create for us.

Even when there was no proof that it would work, I kept showing up. Not with perfect plans or flawless strategies, but with stubborn, imperfect steps forward. One day, one decision, one act of faith at a time.

The First Big Win

With my back against the wall, I knew I couldn't keep doing what I'd been doing. The endless launches that barely broke even, the scattered free content that took so much energy but gave so little back—it wasn't working. Something had to change, and fast.

One morning, I sat down and asked myself a question: *What can I create and sell right now that will bring in cash—immediately?*

I flipped back through a brainstorming list I'd created months earlier during a session with my mentor. It was full of half-formed ideas, most of which didn't feel right. But one stood out: sales training.

I'd already taught thousands of women how to sell through my online courses. Sales was a skill I understood inside and out. And before launching Career Girl, I had years of retail experience. I knew the world these teams were working in—the pressure to hit numbers, the dynamic between managers and sales staff, the stress of the sales floor.

It wasn't flashy or trendy. But it could work. And at the time, I needed something that could work.

So, I decided to pitch it.

I sent a short, straightforward email to a few stores, including the country manager of Lindex, one of the largest retail chains in Finland. Honestly, I didn't expect much. I figured she might ignore it or politely decline. To my surprise, she replied almost immediately: "Call me."

I didn't hesitate and called right away. When she picked up, I spoke from the heart. I told her what I'd noticed about her stores, what her teams were struggling with, and how I could help. I explained my vision for a pilot training program I was looking to test—one that wouldn't just teach techniques, but would give her staff real confidence in how they interact with customers.

She invited me to meet, and after that first meeting, they agreed to pilot my training in a few stores. The results spoke for themselves. Soon, they asked for more, and before long, I was training all the sales managers in Finland, and eventually, across the Baltics.

That first contract was worth around $4,400. It wasn't a fortune, but it proved there was demand for what I could deliver and gave me the energy to keep going. With Lindex on board, I pitched to other companies—beauty salons, pharmacies, boutique retailers—any team that needed help building their sales skills. One by one, they signed on.

Soon, I was standing in rooms full of women in their twenties and thirties, teaching them how to sell in a way that felt authentic and empowering. These weren't just skills—they were life tools.

And here's some irony for you: My mentor at the time told me this idea would never work. "How are you going to compete with men who've been doing this for twenty years?" he asked. But I wasn't competing. I was creating something entirely new: a training designed for women, by a woman, rooted in understanding rather than intimidation.

When those first Lindex sessions took off, I finally had proof that my vision worked. It wasn't recurring revenue yet, and it wasn't fully scalable, but it was real traction. In just three months, I went from $7,300 in the red to $10,000 in profit. For the first time, I could pay myself a real salary.

More than that, I proved to myself that I could turn a business around, even from the toughest circumstances.

Believe Before You See It

The early stages of building a business are messy, uncertain, and often lonely. You're taking action without proof, investing time and money without guarantees, and showing up for a future no one else can see yet. It's natural to crave evidence before you fully commit. Testimonials, revenue, external validation—all of these make it easier to believe you're on the right track.

But in entrepreneurship, belief must come first.

You don't wait for proof before you believe. You believe so deeply that your actions create the proof.

This isn't just mindset fluff. It's the foundation of how sustainable businesses are built. That's why it's the first chapter. Without belief, every setback feels like a sign to quit. Every failed launch feels like proof you're not cut out for this. But when you cultivate belief as a discipline, you stay grounded through the inevitable ups and downs. You keep moving, even when nothing seems to be working.

When I was at my lowest—overdrawn, exhausted, unsure how to pay my bills—there was no external evidence that my business would succeed. The only thing I had was my vision and a quiet, persistent voice saying, *Keep going.*

Over time, I learned that belief isn't just something you feel. It's something you *practice*. And like any practice, it gets stronger the more you use it. Here are the core principles that carried me through my own struggle season and helped me finally reach my first big breakthrough.

Vision Over Timeline

Early on, I made the mistake of tying my worth to deadlines. I'd tell myself,

By spring, I'll hit this revenue goal.

By summer, I'll hire this team member.

By year-end, everything will fall into place.

But when those milestones came and went without the results I had imagined, it was super disappointing. I began to question my abilities and even my dream itself.

Looking back, I realize that I was trying to measure long-term growth on a short-term timeline. Even then, I knew this business was different from my first one. Back in 2017, I had simply created a job for myself, something I could spin up quickly and run solo. But now, with a bigger vision and higher stakes, I was building something that would take time, structure, and patience. I reminded myself that I wasn't just trying to survive the next three months—I was building something for the long haul.

Much later, I came across a quote from Myron Golden: "Goals with timelines often just make us upset." That resonated with me because it captured what I had already lived through during this early stage. I was setting deadlines that didn't match the reality of what I was trying to build. Eventually, I stopped obsessing over *when* things would happen and started focusing on *why* I was doing it.

In the following chapters, you will see long-term thinking come up again and again. It's a crucial mindset to adopt. When you adopt long-term thinking, you'll see a paradox come to play: When you loosen your grip on the timeline, things often happen faster. Isn't that funny? Without the constant pressure to "hurry up and succeed," you'll make clearer, more strategic decisions. You'll stop chasing quick fixes and start laying the groundwork for sustainable growth.

Train Your Brain to See Progress

One of the most dangerous beliefs in business is that progress only counts when it shows up in numbers. If you're not seeing big revenue jumps or massive audience growth, it's easy to convince yourself you're failing.

But growth is often invisible long before it becomes obvious.

During my hardest months, I made a deliberate choice to find a lesson from every failure. For example, when a webinar flopped, I'd study the numbers to see where people dropped off. Around that time, I also started journaling, not as a formal practice, but as a way to process what I was learning. Later, this habit turned into a daily ritual: writing three wins from the day and three I wanted to create tomorrow. It helped me see progress I would have likely otherwise missed.

This reflection kept me motivated and reminded me that when external results were slow, internal growth was happening. I was becoming a different person, a stronger leader, a better business owner.

Progress isn't always visible. But if you train yourself to see it, you'll stay in motion long enough for the visible results to arrive.

Stay Steady Through Highs and Lows

Entrepreneurship is emotional whiplash. One morning, you land a dream client. That afternoon, you get a refund request.

If you let every high and low dictate your mood, you'll burn out fast.

Someone once told me: "Don't get too high on the highs or too low on the lows." It sounded simple, but it became a mantra for me. I'll admit, I'm not great at celebrating wins, even though I constantly remind my clients to do so. For me, growing a business has always felt like playing a game I love. I show up every day wanting to level up, not to chase a particular feeling.

Over time, I've trained myself not to take things personally. When something flopped, I didn't spiral. I asked, *What can I learn here?* and moved on. The more problems I faced, the easier it became to stay calm and objective. This steadiness gave me clarity. Instead of reacting emotionally to every little thing, I focused on the bigger picture. Over time, that stability compounded. It allowed me to make better decisions and keep showing up, even when the external results didn't match the internal effort.

Take It One Day at a Time

Some seasons, the only strategy I had was this: *Just get through the day.*

There were stretches when my goals felt impossibly far away and my issues list felt endless. During those times, thinking about "forever" or even "next month" was overwhelming. So I brought my focus back to the smallest possible unit of progress: today.

Could I keep going for one more day?

Could I show up for my clients today?

Could I make one more call, send one more pitch, try one more thing?

That was enough.

Day by day, action by action, I kept going. Eventually, one day, I realized it didn't feel so hard anymore. The challenges were still there, but they no longer felt overwhelming. By taking it one day at a time, I had worked my way through that season.

The Discipline of Belief

Belief isn't a one-time decision. It's a muscle you build by repeatedly choosing to trust yourself and your vision—even without any visible movement. There were days when my belief felt unshakable, and days when it was barely a whisper.

Belief looked like showing up to a webinar even when only five people registered. It looked like pitching a new offer when I wasn't yet sure I could deliver the results I wanted for clients. It looked like posting a video or going live without knowing if anyone would watch, comment, or care.

Over and over again, I acted *as if* my future success was inevitable. Not because I was certain, but because I was committed. And that's what belief really is: a commitment to your vision, long before the world catches up to it.

When you approach your business this way, you stop chasing external validation. You stop waiting for someone else to tell you you're ready. You take bold, intentional action, and you create the momentum that leads to your breakthrough.

Key Takeaways

#1. Believe before you see proof.
Any time you set out to reach a goal you haven't achieved before, there's uncertainty. That's normal. The key is to believe in your vision long before the results are visible. When doubt creeps in, look for proof from others who've already done it—it's evidence that it's possible for you too. That belief becomes the fuel that keeps you going when external validation hasn't shown up yet.

#2. Clarity comes through action, not waiting.
You don't need a perfect plan to start. The act of building, launching, and iterating gives you the insights you can't get from thinking alone. Progress comes from moving, not waiting to feel ready.

#3. One strong offer is more powerful than many small ones.
Instead of scattering your energy across endless small products, focus on creating one meaningful offer that truly serves your audience. This focus gives you leverage and simplifies your path to growth.

#4. Self-doubt is part of the journey.
Feeling like an outsider doesn't mean you're on the wrong path—it often means you're creating a new one. Every entrepreneur struggles in the

beginning, even if it looks effortless from the outside. The key is to keep going, surround yourself with stories of others who've been where you are, and remember that growth often feels uncomfortable because you're building something that hasn't existed before.

#5. Resilience is built in the struggle.
The hard seasons—the red numbers, the failed launches, the "almost there" moments—are what shape you into the kind of leader who can succeed. They're preparing you for the breakthrough ahead. When your business struggles, it's teaching you. When it thrives, you're teaching it.

Strategies & Tools

Believing in yourself is a skill you can strengthen. Here are some practical ways to build unshakable belief, even when the results haven't shown up yet:

Shifting Your Identity

Your vision for the future has to feel real long before it shows up in your numbers. The point isn't just to repeat affirmation—it's to embody the person who already lives in the life you're working toward.

For me, that means stepping into my "Millionaire Marianne" identity every day. I've written statements that describe how she thinks, leads, and makes decisions. These are more than just motivational quotes too. They are identity-based commitments that shape how I act. When I read them each morning, I'm reminding myself who I am becoming and guiding my choices through that version of me.

One of my favorites is: "I'm building a solid, long-term business, and because of that, everything I want will come to me at the right time."

Another one: "I have permission to set boundaries. I leave messages unanswered without guilt, because focus is my most important resource."

This practice is intended to train your brain to operate from your next level *now*. Over time, it builds confidence. I also keep two vision boards side by side: one that shows my future goals, and another that reminds me of everything I've already achieved. Looking at both reinforces my belief that if I've reached all of this already, I'll naturally reach the next level too.

Create a personal manifesto of your own. Write down a few identity-based commitments that will anchor you in who you're becoming. These statements should reflect the leader you want to be and the future you're building. Read your manifesto every morning and every night. This repetition rewires your thinking, especially on tough days when self-doubt creeps in. Over time, this practice helps you build what I call your *Premium Persona*—the version of you who already operates at the level you're working toward.

And one more thought: This kind of mindset work is not about positive thinking. It's about discipline and showing up as the person who's already achieved what you're building. When your identity shifts first, the results eventually follow.

Think 10x, Not 2x

One of the mindset tools that helped me in scaling my business comes from *10x Is Easier Than 2x* by Dan Sullivan and Dr. Benjamin Hardy. The book flips traditional growth thinking on its head. Aiming for 10x growth doesn't mean working harder or doing more; it means thinking differently. When your goal is that big, you can't rely on small tweaks or longer hours. You have to redesign how you work: your systems, your environment, your priorities, and even your identity.

This idea helped me expand what I thought was possible and find creative solutions I wouldn't have seen if I was only trying to double something. It also changed how I lead my team because 10x thinking forces you to identify the few activities that truly move the needle (the ones matched to your unique strengths) and delegate or eliminate the rest.

It also forces you to think long term. My coach Peter once told me something that shifted everything for me and helped me believe in my big 10x goals: "It's not the goals that are unrealistic—it's the timelines." That one sentence gave me permission to zoom out. Instead of asking,

"Can I do this in one to three years?" I started asking, "Am I willing to let this take fifteen to twenty-five years if it has to?" That question calmed my nervous system and expanded my thinking at the same time. When you give your brain that much room, you suddenly see possibilities and strategies you couldn't see when you were squeezing everything into a short deadline. And ironically, once you map out the long-term plan, you often realize it probably won't take that long.

It's a simple reframe: Let go of everything that only leads to 2x growth so you can focus your time and energy on what creates 10x results.

The 3 Wins Journal

Progress is built one day at a time, and it's easy to lose sight of how far you've come when you're focused only on what's not working. Each night, take a few minutes to write down three wins from today—no matter how small—and three wins you want for tomorrow. This simple practice does two things:

- It forces you to recognize your progress and celebrate momentum, which builds confidence.
- It shifts your focus from problems to possibilities, helping you wake up with clarity and purpose.

Hindsight tip: I wish I had done this from the very beginning. It's one of those habits that seems small, but over time, it changes how you approach your work and your growth, so start now.

Choose Your Inputs Wisely

The voices you listen to shape how you see yourself and what you believe is possible. It's not just about the five people you spend the most time with—it's also about the five voices you let into your mind every day.

Pay attention to what you're consuming. Podcasts, books, social media—these all shape your perspective. But don't just listen passively. Study the people who are currently living the life or running the kind of business you want. Investigate *why* they've succeeded. In most cases, it's not because they're doing dramatically more but because they've learned what *not* to do.

When you hear someone else's success, don't compare yourself to their current stage. Instead, look at where they were at your level. That's where the real insight lives. Use their journey as a roadmap. If someone has already done what you want to do, it's proof that it can be done again.

You are not special in your struggles or limitations. The good news is that the path to your breakthrough already exists. The more you surround yourself with stories of people who've done what you want to do, the more inevitable your own success will feel.

These tools may seem simple, but when practiced consistently, they compound over time. They help you show up as the leader your business needs, not just once in a while, but every day.

Final Thoughts

In the beginning, belief was all I had.

When my mentor told me I could build a million-dollar business, it felt so far beyond my current reality that I almost laughed. At the time, I didn't have proof—no steady income, no scalable product, no sign that what I was building would work. What I *did* have was a vision I couldn't shake and the willingness to keep showing up for it, day after day, even when no one else could see it.

Those early years weren't glamorous. They were marked by long nights, failed launches, and more nos than I can count. I was in the red, questioning myself constantly, and frustrated to the point of exhaustion. I kept asking myself, *When is it going to be time? Isn't it supposed to be now? When will my breakthrough finally happen?*

But every time I felt like walking away, I remembered why I started. I was on a mission. From the very beginning, this business was born out of a calling to help women achieve more and to give them permission to be unapologetically ambitious. I still remember the exact moment I realized it in 2019. I thought to myself, *This is it. This is what I'm going to do for the rest of my life.* It felt so powerful.

That's also why quitting never crossed my mind. Deep down, I knew I would make it work somehow—I just didn't know how yet. Looking back, maybe that entire first chapter of my journey wasn't about failure at all. It was about learning. I didn't know the right business model or the right offer. That was the real problem, not my ability.

Believing in yourself before you have evidence isn't easy. It's messy and humbling. But it's also what separates those who stay stuck from those who eventually break through.

In the next chapter, we'll dive into that first big breakthrough—how it unfolded, why it mattered, and what it taught me about turning belief into momentum.

CHAPTER 2
THE FIRST BIG BREAKTHROUGH

My friend's words landed like a punch to the gut.

"Marianne, you could be making a way bigger impact if you focused on entrepreneurs again. People who want this. People like you."

On paper, things were finally working. After years of struggling to find stability, I had a premium offer that was selling. Money was coming in. For the first time, the numbers looked good instead of terrifying. But beneath that relief was a gnawing feeling I couldn't ignore: Something about this wasn't right.

I had been spending my days driving to retail stores, masked up, delivering sales trainings to teams of employees who hadn't chosen to be there. They were polite and respectful, but I could feel it—most of them saw this as just another meeting to get through before their lunch break. They weren't lit up by the material. They weren't hungry to change anything.

And if I'm honest, neither was I.

Was I grateful? Of course. Grateful that we weren't in the red anymore, grateful that I'd finally figured out how to make real money doing something I was good at. But this wasn't why I started Career Girl. This wasn't the mission that had pulled me in all those years ago.

In my rush to keep the lights on, I had drifted.

That's why my friend's comment hit me so hard. Because she was right. I hadn't built this business for people who were just clocking in for a paycheck. I built it for ambitious women who were creating something of their own, who had fire in their eyes and visions that kept them up at night. Women like me.

At the time, I was still focused on figuring out how to scale the sales training side of the business. I explored building an app, looked into the startup world, and even started researching how to get investors. But none of it felt right. I didn't change anything right away, but my friend's words planted a seed I couldn't ignore.

Things then shifted when I completed a mindset training with Sam Ovens's online course—a $400 Black Friday purchase. That's when I realized I could combine what I'd learned from the B2B and premium-offer world with the online course model and create a high-level program for my real audience: entrepreneurs.

And that's when I finally found my breakthrough.

In this chapter, we'll look at how to find and create your first true breakthrough—the moment when your offer, audience, and message finally come together. You'll see how small, simple tests can validate your idea, why confidence comes from action instead of perfection, and how focus can turn early wins into sustainable growth.

Finding the Breakthrough

After that moment of clarity, I didn't change everything overnight, but I did start looking for ways to bring what I'd learned about premium offers into the entrepreneurial space. I was looking for my breakthrough. Around that time, I was following another online coach who had hosted a one-day VIP workshop for her audience. The idea clicked immediately, so I decided to model it. I used her email content as a starting point, wrote my own version, and adapted it to my audience.

This was actually my second time running a VIP day. I'd tested something similar about six months earlier, but this time, I wanted to give it another shot because I had more clarity on who it was for. The idea was simple: Host a one-day in-person workshop in Helsinki for course creators and small business owners who wanted to move beyond low-priced offers and start selling something more premium. I called it the In-Demand Offer.

I booked a small co-working space in Helsinki, set up some snacks, and prepared a short presentation. Nothing polished, just a solid framework and the kind of hands-on session I would've wanted to attend myself. Then I posted about it on social media and sent one direct email to my list.

To my surprise, ten people signed up—nine women and one man—each paying $500.

That day felt so refreshing compared to the corporate trainings. These people weren't there because their boss made them show up. They *wanted* to be there. They were engaged, excited, and deeply invested in what they were learning. Their energy was contagious.

For the first time in a long time, I felt connected to what mattered again.

As I watched them lean forward in their chairs, asking questions and brainstorming ideas, I realized how much I'd missed this kind of work. This was why I'd started Career Girl in the first place: to help ambitious people like me create something meaningful for themselves and their families.

After the energy of that first workshop, I couldn't stop thinking about what had happened in that room. Ten people had shown up ready to work, ready to take action—and that told me something important: There was a real demand for this kind of workshop by people who wanted to be coached. The VIP day ended up becoming the validation for another idea I had already created and started selling: the *Instant Growth Accelerator*, a high-touch program for course creators ready to move beyond low-ticket offers and finally build something sustainable.

At the beginning of 2022, I had set a clear goal for myself: This year, I wanted to make $100,000 in a single month. From Sam Ovens's course, I'd learned that the path to big results was focus—doing one thing and doing it exceptionally well. The only missing piece was figuring out how to attract high-ticket clients.

Ovens's model relied on paid ads, but that wasn't an option for me. I didn't have the budget, and based on my past experiences, I didn't trust ads to bring the kind of clients I wanted anyway. So, I did what any entrepreneur does when they hit a wall: I opened Google and searched: *how to sell high-ticket offers organically without ads.*

That's when I found another coach's program that promised exactly that. I booked a sales call, and they quoted $15,000, split into three installments. Whoa. The price tag was hard to swallow, but I believed it was what I needed. Looking at my finances, I could afford the first payment and was fairly confident I could manage the second, but I had no idea how I'd cover the third.

Which meant one thing: I had no choice but to make it work.

When I joined the program, my goal was simple: to get five clients to sign up for *Instant Growth Accelerator*. Five felt ambitious but manageable. Since I ran my previous sales training as a pilot, I decided to do the same here. I launched it as a beta version at a discounted price of $2,000. From the start, I was transparent with my audience about this being a beta. They knew the twelve-week program would evolve and improve as we went, and that in future rounds, the price would increase significantly. That created excitement and urgency: They weren't just buying into the program—they were getting in early at a special rate.

I didn't have branding, a polished website, or a team to back me up. I sold through conversations and posts. I wanted to talk to as many people as possible, so I borrowed other audiences by pitching myself to run webinars for established communities, opened as many conversations as I could, and filled my calendar with calls. My only goal was to get in front of the right people, explain what I was building, and personally invite them to join the beta program.

To generate interest, I posted in a large Finnish entrepreneur group of over 60,000 members. My post was straightforward and honest—no hype, no heavy sales language. I described the exact kind of person the program was for and the problem it would solve.

The first few hours were quiet. I had posted in the evening, and when I checked later that night, there were no comments at all. I went to bed thinking, *Okay, that post didn't work. I'll try again tomorrow.*

But the next morning, when I opened Facebook, the post had exploded. Comments began to appear. DMs started flooding in. Questions. Requests for details. Calls being booked. Within days, what had felt like silence turned into a wave of interest.

Now it was time to sell.

THE FIRST BIG BREAKTHROUGH

Before I closed my first deal, I took at least ten, maybe eleven, sales calls. Each one taught me something. I was learning how to describe my offer more clearly, how to manage objections, and how to not take things personally when the call didn't end with a yes. My sales coach at the time told me something important: "Your first ten to fifteen calls with a new offer are just practice. Don't expect anything from them." She was right, and that mindset kept me grounded. I didn't see the early nos as failures—they were data points.

When I finally closed my first client at $2,000, it felt incredible. That was the turning point. Once I'd done it once, I knew I could do it again. The momentum picked up quickly from there, and soon more clients started joining.

By the time enrollment closed, *thirty people had signed up*—twenty-nine Finnish speakers and one English speaker. It was six times my original goal.

I was stunned.

I had been prepared to work closely with five clients, building the program as we went. Now I had thirty people counting on me. The workload instantly multiplied: more coaching calls, more resources to create, more support to provide.

I'll be honest. It was definitely overwhelming, but it didn't feel heavy. For the first time, there was *real demand*. These people weren't hesitant or skeptical. They were ready, eager, and willing to invest in themselves. And because they knew they were part of a special beta round, they were deeply engaged and excited to help shape the experience.

Moreover, this product was proof of *product-market fit*—that powerful moment when your offer perfectly matches with what your audience needs and is actively seeking. For years, I had been trying to create momentum through sheer effort. Now, for the first time, it felt like the market was pulling me forward. Selling wasn't a battle. It was a natural extension of serving the right people with the right offer.

That single launch didn't just validate the program—it eventually changed the direction of my business. It marked the moment I began transitioning from Career Girl to what eventually became Smart Mentoring—with a sharper niche, a more defined target market, and a clearer way of delivering results.

As I dove into delivering that first round, I made a promise to myself: No matter how many people joined, I would show up fully for every single one of them. These thirty people had trusted me with their businesses and their dreams. In return, I would give them everything I had, not just to help them succeed, but to refine the program into something truly scalable.

That round of *Instant Growth Accelerator* wasn't perfect. Some trainings were messy, some calls went off track, and many resources were created on the fly. But the people inside the program got results, and I learned more in those weeks than I had in years of trial and error.

What was even more exciting was that I could clearly see the path forward. This wasn't about chasing one-off wins anymore. It was proof that I finally had something I could scale—something with real impact that I could grow, expand, and eventually build a team around.

It was my first, official breakthrough.

Suddenly, I had proof that my vision wasn't just a dream. It was real. I felt like I had made it.

How to Work for a Breakthrough

A breakthrough doesn't just come from thinking differently; it comes from *working differently*. The way you approach your work determines how quickly you grow, how you handle challenges, and whether you ever reach the point where everything finally clicks.

My breakthrough started when I stopped doing most of the things I thought *I should* be doing. I said no to opportunities that didn't match my vision. I turned down job offers that would have brought short-term money but would have distracted me from my long-term goals. Instead, I focused all my energy on one thing: building and selling the program that would take me where I wanted to go. I realized that saying no is one of the hardest and most important skills you can build as an entrepreneur.

You can't scale if you're all over the place.

You don't need a perfect brand, a big team, or elaborate tech systems to create a breakthrough. What you need is clarity about who you serve, the willingness to connect deeply with them, and the discipline to stay focused on what matters most. The following practices helped me reshape how *I worked*. They're simple actions that help you grow without getting lost in overplanning and perfectionism. When you apply them consistently, you create the right conditions for your own breakthrough.

Start Simple and Sell Through Conversations

When you're just starting out—or pivoting to a new offer—the fastest way to validate an idea isn't with a sales page, funnel, or ad campaign. It's through conversations.

Go where your ideal clients are already spending time: Facebook groups, Instagram, LinkedIn, or even your existing network. Start talking about the problem you solve and the transformation you deliver. When someone shows interest, reach out personally with a direct message or a quick voice note.

This moves beyond selling because it's more about connection. Listen to their struggles. Instead of pitching right away, try to figure out what they actually need. Share how you can help. Regardless of how many likes or comments you get online, the clearest sign that your idea is working is when someone says yes on a discovery call and invests in themselves.

When I first launched *Instant Growth Accelerator*, I didn't even have a full website, only a simple landing page (and I've learned that you don't even need that). My only focus was on having real conversations, which allowed me to refine my message in real time and build trust quickly.

Protect Your Focus Like It's Sacred

Breakthroughs require your attention. That means saying no to anything that doesn't directly support your core offer or your growth. That's why, during this season, I suggest you commit to a "monk-like" focus. Temporarily step away from distractions like coffee chats, side projects, or exciting opportunities that don't support your bigger vision.

This isn't forever. It's about creating the mental and physical space you need to fully commit to selling, serving, and refining your signature program. When I protected my time this way, I was able to use my energy wisely.

Speak Your Goals into Reality

One of the simplest practices that helped me create my first breakthrough was speaking my goals out loud. When you say your goals only in your head, they stay abstract and safe. When you *speak* them—whether it's to a client, your team, or someone you trust—they become real. Suddenly, there's accountability. Every decision you make is filtered through that vision, and you can no longer hide from it.

I learned this lesson during the very first session of *Instant Growth Accelerator*. At the end of a call, I took a deep breath and said to the beta group, "I want to create a $100,000 month." It felt incredibly awkward. My face was hot, and part of me wanted to take it back the second I said it. I worried they'd think it was naive or overconfident. But instead of judgment, I saw nods of support.

In that moment, the goal stopped being a private dream and became a shared vision. From then on, every move I made—every decision, every risk, every yes or no—was shaped by that goal.

This is why I encourage you to try it too. Speak your vision out loud, even if it makes you uncomfortable. Start small. Share it with one person you trust or with a small group of clients. That simple act can change how you show up and give you the courage to take bold action.

Mindset Shifts That Make Breakthroughs Possible

While the last section was about your approach to work, this one is about your mindset—the beliefs and perspectives that shape every decision you make. Every strategy in the world won't matter if your mindset isn't moving you toward where you want to go. Breakthroughs aren't just external events—they're internal transformations. The way you think shapes the decisions you make, the risks you take, and ultimately, the results you achieve.

The following mindset shifts are the ones I now teach my clients to help them move forward boldly, even when things feel messy or uncertain. These are the shifts that turn hesitation into momentum and vision into reality.

Confidence Is Built Through Action

Most entrepreneurs think they need confidence before they can take big steps—launching a new offer, raising their prices, or showing up publicly. The truth is, confidence comes from *doing*.

Every no, every imperfect attempt, every messy first version is part of building self-trust. Instead of seeing rejection or failure as proof you're not ready, view it as practice. Each conversation, each sale (or non-sale), is data you can use to improve.

You don't need to have it all figured out before you start. You need to start in order to figure it out. Think of confidence like a muscle. You don't get stronger by reading about lifting weights. You get stronger by lifting, failing, and trying again.

Bigger Results Require Bigger Thinking

If your goals stay small, your actions will stay small. You'll naturally build systems, pricing, and strategies that match where you are now and not where you want to go. But when you set a vision that feels bigger than your current capacity, you begin making decisions from your future level, not your current one.

For me, this became clear the moment I committed to my first truly bold goal: generating $100,000 in a single month. At the time, it felt almost unreasonable. The year before, in 2021, my business had brought in around $80,000 total. Setting that larger goal forced me to think, act, and lead differently. I raised my prices. I raised my standards. I narrowed my focus to the few activities that truly moved the business forward. I couldn't get there by doing things the same way I had always done them.

That bigger goal demanded a bigger version of me.

When I changed my actions to match that level of thinking, the business responded. In the following year, revenue grew to approximately $900,000. That's an increase of more than 1,000 percent. Talk about a breakthrough! It was the result of expanded perspective, clearer decisions, and consistent execution.

The results you want won't come from staying who you've been. They come from expanding how you think and allowing that expansion to guide your decisions long before you see the evidence. Bigger thinking leads to bigger decisions—and bigger decisions create bigger outcomes.

Sustainability Comes from Refinement, Not Reinvention

Many entrepreneurs fall into the trap of constantly creating new offers, programs, or products to keep things "fresh." They fear that repeating the same offer will get boring—for them or their clients.

I know this trap well because I did exactly that. In my early days, I kept creating new courses and offers every month, thinking innovation was the only way to grow. But all it really did was scatter my focus and leave me exhausted, always chasing the next big idea instead of building on what was already working.

In order to scale your business, you don't have to reinvent the wheel every few months. It comes from refining what works. Each time you run the same offer, you gain insights and make improvements. The delivery becomes smoother, the client results deepen, and your systems strengthen. Stability means having a strong foundation you can grow from without burning yourself out.

Key Takeaways

#1. Breakthroughs come from clarity, not hustle.

Your breakthrough happens when your offer, audience, and message come together, not when you push harder. When you focus on the right people and the right problem, selling becomes natural and sustainable.

#2. **Find product-market fit before you scale.**
Scaling only works when your offer matches what your audience deeply wants and needs. My one-day VIP workshop revealed strong demand and became the foundation for a high-ticket program. You don't need a perfect launch—you need proof that the market is ready and eager for your solution.

#3. **Confidence is built through action.**
You don't need to feel ready before you start. I launched *Instant Growth Accelerator* without a website or branding. Taking imperfect action—and learning as I went—built the confidence I needed to keep going.

#4. **Focus creates momentum.**
When you say no to distractions and stay committed to one clear offer, growth accelerates. Monk-like focus helped me refine and scale *Instant Growth Accelerator* quickly without burning out.

#5. **Refine, don't reinvent.**
In order to grow, you don't have to be constantly innovating. You just have to stick with an idea long enough for it to work. Each round of delivery helps you strengthen systems and deepen client results without starting over.

Strategies & Tools

While my approach to work and mindset were crucial in creating my breakthrough, the systems I built around them were just as important. Even simple tools gave me the structure to turn early wins into something repeatable. The next two frameworks—one for pricing and one for positioning—were the foundation of my early growth. They helped me define my value, communicate it clearly, and sell my offer with confidence, and they're the first tools I now teach clients when they're building something high-ticket.

High-Ticket Pricing Framework

One of the biggest shifts in my business came when I stopped creating low-cost offers for everyone and instead built a premium program for a very specific type of client. I focused on a single, tangible transformation that deeply mattered to my audience. When you know exactly who you're serving and what problem you're solving, you can confidently price your offer at a high-ticket level. High pricing is about reflecting the depth of the result and the level of support you provide, not just inflating value.

A simple tool I now teach for defining premium pricing is something I call the Dream Testimonial Method. It helps you clarify your outcome, understand where the value truly comes from, and confidently price your program based on transformation and not the number of calls, worksheets, or modules inside it.

Here's how you do it:

Step 1: Write your dream testimonial. What would your dream client say about your program if they achieved the absolute best possible result? Write it in their voice as if it has already happened. To guide your writing, consider the following:

- What did they find most valuable?
- What concrete change happened in their business or life?
- How would they describe the transformation in simple, everyday language?
- What problem do they no longer struggle with?
- What was the moment they thought, *This was worth every dollar*?

Step 2: Extract the real outcome. Read your dream testimonial and circle one to three concrete results, such as:

- "I enrolled my first five premium clients."
- "I stopped freelancing and built a real delivery system."
- "I gained clarity, confidence, and consistent revenue."
- "I finally stepped into a CEO identity."

These become your program's promised transformation, the reason your offer is premium, and the core of your marketing message. Once you extract the true outcome, your offer becomes clearer (and so does the value).

Step 3: Price the transformation, not the work. Once you know the transformation, ask yourself the following:

- If someone truly achieved this result, what would it be worth to them over the next twelve months (financially, emotionally, in time saved, in identity shifts)?
- How much would it cost them to keep trying this alone for another year?
- What price honestly reflects the depth of this transformation (and not the amount of work you'll do)?

For most people, their premium price lands within these ranges:

- $3,000–$15,000 (B2C)
- $8,000–$30,000 (B2B)

This method removes the guesswork. Instead of trying to justify a price based on "deliverables," you anchor your pricing to the transformation your client actually cares about.

Crafting a Clear, High-Ticket Positioning Statement

The second tool that shaped my breakthrough was learning how to articulate my offer with absolute clarity. Before I could confidently sell a premium program, I needed a positioning statement that captured who I served, what result I delivered, and why it mattered. A clear "I help" statement becomes the backbone of your marketing and sales—it sharpens your message, attracts the right people, and instantly communicates the value of your offer. One simple method we now use is the 3-Step High-Ticket Positioning Framework.

This is how it works:

Step 1: Find the polarity. Start by understanding the emotional journey your ideal client is on. Take a piece of paper and draw two columns. In the first column, list ten things they're moving away from. These could be things like undercharging, overwhelm, inconsistent income, unclear messaging, lack of systems, fear of selling, burnout, generic offers, the freelancer mindset, lack of confidence, and so on. In the second column, list ten things they're moving toward. Maybe it's premium pricing, clear positioning, consistent revenue, the CEO identity, scalable systems, confidence, higher-value clients, stability, or bigger opportunities. This polarity map gives you clarity on the gap your offer closes.

Step 2: Write three positioning statements. Using the polarity map as inspiration, now write three variations of your "I help" statement using this template:

I help [WHO] to [RESULT] so that they [MEANINGFUL OUTCOME].

For example: "I help experienced experts build a premium offer that consistently sells for $5,000–$15,000 so they can create stable, predictable revenue." Write three versions even if one feels obvious. Write three versions even if one feels good right away. Exploring different angles often reveals a stronger, sharper message than the one you started with.

Step 3: Test in real contexts. Put each version into circulation and observe how people respond. Test them in conversations, DMs, story slides, your bio, short intro messages, LinkedIn posts, or even on sales calls. Notice which version makes people say, "I need this," which one feels most natural to say out loud, which is clearest to someone who doesn't know you, which sparks follow-up questions, and which makes your ideal client feel genuinely seen. The statement that consistently draws curiosity and resonance is your winning one.

This simple positioning framework makes selling your offer far easier. When you can communicate your value in one sharp, meaningful sentence, you create instant clarity for yourself and for the people you're here to help.

Final Thoughts

When my friend said, "Marianne, you could be making a way bigger impact if you focused on entrepreneurs again," it felt like a challenge and a reminder all at once. She'd helped me realize how far I'd drifted from my original vision, and how much I wanted to come back to the work that truly lit me up.

That conversation eventually led me to finding a product-market fit—my first official breakthrough.

But breakthroughs don't make things easy. In fact, they often bring new challenges. Going from five expected clients to thirty meant more moving parts, more pressure, and more responsibility than I'd ever handled before. Suddenly, I wasn't just coaching a handful of clients—I was running a program that needed structure, systems, and support.

This is the part most people don't talk about. You fight so hard to get to the breakthrough moment, but once you're there, a new reality sets in: delivering on results you promised. Breakthroughs get clients in the door, but fulfillment is what actually transforms them—and what ultimately builds your brand. In the next chapter, we'll dive into how to deliver results at scale through a product- and client-fulfillment system that creates consistent, repeatable transformation.

CHAPTER 3

PRODUCT AND CLIENT FULFILLMENT—DELIVERING RESULTS AT SCALE

A business grows on the strength of what it delivers. When your product works—and I mean *really works*—it becomes the center of your reputation, your referrals, and your long-term stability. Clients don't remember the branding, the website, or the polish. They remember the moment something finally clicked, the moment they saw progress, or the moment your work changed something for them.

Those outcomes don't happen by accident. They come from a product built with intention and a fulfillment system designed to support people through real transformation. As your business grows, the ability to deliver predictable results becomes the difference between momentum and stagnation. The clients who thrive inside your product create a ripple effect: stronger testimonials, deeper trust, and a community of people who believe in your work because they've lived it.

One of the most common hesitations I hear from clients is this: "How could I possibly promise a clear outcome when life is so uncertain?" It's an honest, thoughtful question. After all, no one can control timing, circumstances, or the personal variables each client brings into the process. For many people, the idea of clearly naming an outcome feels risky, even reckless—as if doing so might set them (and their clients) up for disappointment.

But in practice, promising an outcome is not the same as guaranteeing a specific, uncontrollable result. What you are really committing to is the integrity of your process. A well-built, well-delivered product creates the conditions for transformation: clear steps, consistent support, and an environment where progress becomes far more likely than stagnation.

This chapter shows you how to design those conditions intentionally—so that offering a clear outcome no longer feels like guesswork, but a grounded, responsible extension of the work you already know how to do. You'll learn how to structure a product that creates meaningful results, how to support clients in a way that protects your energy, how to filter for the people who are the best fit for your process, and how to build systems that make fulfillment feel steady and scalable.

These foundations give your business something rare: a path where results are repeatable, clients stay engaged, and your product becomes known for the transformation it creates.

Building My Product

When I first launched my program, thirty people trusted me with their goals—thirty real humans with real expectations—and I felt the weight of that immediately. It was exhilarating, but it was also the moment I realized I had crossed a line: This wasn't an idea anymore. I had to deliver, and deliver well.

But—and this part is a little unnerving—I didn't even know if my process would work!

I literally had zero evidence that I would get my clients any results at all. What I *did* know, however, was that I would commit. I made the decision to go all in, no matter what. I promised myself that if someone showed up and did the work, I would make sure they got to the finish line, even if it took longer than expected. That commitment became the backbone of my fulfillment philosophy: A product shouldn't just promise results—it should be structured in a way that *creates* them.

Pretty quickly, though, once clients started hitting their goals, I saw firsthand that the process *did work*. (Phew!) From there, it wasn't about whether my framework was solid anymore—it was about how committed clients were to implementing it. Some didn't do the work and stalled out. Others showed up consistently and got incredible results.

In my case, the group model accelerated everything. Because I ran that first round as a true cohort, everyone began together, moved through the material together, and held one another accountable. That shared energy created momentum. While my beta clients showed up for themselves, they also showed up for the group, and that accountability made the transformation feel bigger than their individual goals.

In those early days, nothing was pre-recorded. Everything was live. Weekly Zoom calls, Q&As, coaching sessions—I was teaching, observing, refining, and immediately folding the insights back into the program. After each call, I'd take what landed most, turn it into a clearer framework, and slowly build the curriculum piece by piece. It was a ton of work, but the product grew because the beta clients inside helped shape it. Their questions revealed where my system needed tightening; their progress revealed what should become a milestone; their sticking points showed me where fulfillment systems needed to evolve.

By the end of that beta round, I had delivered for thirty people *and* built a structured, scalable product. Not because I sat down to create a perfect curriculum in isolation, but because I was in the trenches with the people I was serving, refining everything in real time.

Looking back, despite the intense workload, I'm grateful I started with that many clients. With only a handful, I wouldn't have seen the patterns, the gaps, or the behaviors that make or break a high-ticket program. That volume gave me the data I needed to build stronger fulfillment systems, clarify who the program was actually for, and design a product that could deliver predictable results at scale.

A lot of entrepreneurs try to protect themselves in the early days by limiting capacity. I understand why—it feels safer. But if your goal is to create a product that truly works for more than a few people at a time, taking on more clients early on can actually be the shortcut. It forces you to commit fully, refine faster, and build something robust enough to support real growth.

And that's the heart of product and fulfillment: clarity in your process, commitment to your clients, and structure that enables both to succeed.

Building a High-Ticket Product That Delivers on Its Promise

In the last chapter, you learned how to define a premium transformation, price it with confidence, and articulate it clearly through your positioning. Now comes the part that actually builds your reputation: delivering that transformation consistently. A high-ticket product isn't defined by price but by its ability to create results at scale. And the more premium you go, the more important structure becomes.

At Smart Mentoring, most of our clients come to us with deep expertise. They know how to help people. What they often don't know is how to translate that expertise into a product that gets predictable results for dozens (or hundreds) of clients at a time. They're used to customizing everything, relying on intuition, or "figuring it out on the call." I'm sure you can relate. While that worked during your selling sessions, it won't work the moment you try to sell *transformation*.

A high-ticket product requires clarity, sequence, and boundaries. Here's how we teach clients to build one.

First, start from the outcome—the very transformation you articulated through your dream testimonial and positioning work from the previous chapter. Your premium price is anchored in a specific result, so your product must be engineered backwards from that outcome. Rather than asking, "Who do I want to help?" ask yourself, "What result can I confidently create, and who is most likely to achieve it?" When the outcome is clear, your ideal client becomes obvious: the person with the readiness, resources, and mindset to achieve that result. It's through this clarity that you'll create consistency.

From there, the next step is turning the transformation into a structured path. Every high-ticket product needs *milestones* that move clients from where they are to where they want to go. Each milestone represents one major step your client must complete to reach the final result and should answer three questions: what they need to understand, what action they need to take, and what counts as proof they've completed it (like a deliverable, a result, or a specific action). Only give clients the minimum necessary information to achieve the next step and nothing extra.

This structure protects your clients from overwhelm and keeps the momentum up. You should aim to get the first milestone achieved as quickly as possible. This may surprise you, but premium clients don't want endless videos, hours of content, or complicated workbooks. Most entrepreneurs assume that a high-ticket product requires 100 hours of curriculum, but the opposite is true. Premium clients value momentum over information. They want the shortest, clearest path to the result. Those who crave deep theoretical learning are typically "knowledge collectors," and they're rarely the ones willing to invest at a premium level.

A milestone-based approach keeps clients focused and grounded. They always know exactly what to do next, and they aren't allowed to move to the next phase until they've truly completed the current one.

Once the milestones are set, then comes delivery. Delivery becomes a matter of choosing the simplest, most scalable format. Weekly calls (group or 1:1) paired with basic tools like Google Drive, Notion, Slack, or WhatsApp are more than enough to begin. High-ticket doesn't mean "high complexity." You can build your entire program with simple tools.

Many of our clients start by delivering everything live (just like I did). Once they've taught the same lesson a few times and refined it, they record it and turn it into a module. Over time, their product naturally evolves into a hybrid model that saves time without losing the personalized support that premium buyers expect.

Before scaling, however, the offer and the product must be validated. We never advise running a free beta. Free clients don't commit, and they don't prove demand. Instead, we teach clients to run a paid pilot with a small group of ideal participants at a reduced rate (just like I did). When you do this, you deliver the product in real time, gather feedback, refine the structure, and come out with testimonials, data, and the revenue needed to grow. One round of live delivery often reveals more insight than months of planning.

Finally, fulfillment systems turn a great product into a *scalable* one. Every step of the journey—from sign-up to graduation—should be mapped and supported with simple systems: onboarding messages, first action steps, weekly check-ins, clear communication boundaries, structured feedback loops, and a thoughtful offboarding process.

These systems don't just support the client; they protect the integrity of the product as you grow. With refinement, documentation, and client health tracking, your product becomes something that delivers predictable results without depending entirely on you.

This is how you build a high-ticket product that lives up to its promise. When the outcome is clear, the milestones are simple, the delivery is streamlined, and the systems are strong, your product becomes the foundation of your reputation.

Real Results, Real Fast

At Smart Mentoring, we see this with our clients constantly: Once the transformation is clearly defined, the milestones are mapped, and the offer is positioned around a real outcome—not busywork or endless information—early breakthroughs begin to snowball.

One of our clients, a spiritual transformation coach, was used to the idea that launching required months of funnels, courses, and complicated tech. She was shocked when a single positioning post—rooted in a clear outcome and a simple, milestone-based offer—drew fifty responses, twenty booked calls, and six serious leads, all without spending a single dollar on ads.

The first time she said her new price, $2,500, she thought she might throw up. Saying that number out loud felt terrifying, but because her offer was now anchored in a tangible transformation, she trusted the process, followed the script, and booked her first premium client. That moment gave her the proof she needed. Once she saw that her work created a real, measurable result, her confidence skyrocketed.

This is what happens again and again in our program. Confidence doesn't come from theory—it comes from implementation inside a clear structure. When clients land their first result, their entire identity shifts. They stop hoping their business will work and start *believing* in what they've built.

We've also seen a consistent pattern: As pricing increases, so do results. In the early days, many clients charged less than $2,000. Today, many confidently charge $5,000–$8,000, and the quality of their clients (and the depth of the transformations) has risen with it. When both sides invest more, the structure holds better, the milestones land deeper, and the fulfillment process becomes more powerful.

Take *Mindful Mama*, a program launched by one of our early beta clients. She helped mothers reduce frustration and model healthy emotional habits for their kids. Initially, she planned to run the program for free "just to test it out." She even turned down my early invitation to join our beta because she didn't feel ready.

But when she finally said yes, within her first week she brought in $17,000 in paid clients, all while caring for her baby and working three days a week. And here's the important part: It was the *same* program she'd almost offered for free. The only difference was structure, clarity, and a premium container. And her clients showed up far more powerfully because people who pay, pay attention.

Too often, entrepreneurs assume their ideal clients are the ones who "can't afford it." But premium clients exist in every niche. They want depth, speed, and a proven path. They value their time and see high-quality services as an investment, not a luxury.

All of these stories share one theme: The product wasn't just upgraded on paper. It was *validated* through delivery. When you define the outcome, create the right milestones, support clients through a clear fulfillment system, and work with the people who are ready to implement, real-world results follow. And once those results begin, confidence compounds—for your clients and for you.

The Art of Client Fulfillment Without Over-Responsibility

One of the most misunderstood aspects of scaling a coaching or consulting business is client delivery. Most coaches believe that to guarantee results, they must take on more responsibility. They double their calls, rewrite clients' posts, over-coach, and bend their own systems to meet every emotional reaction along the way.

It comes with good intentions, but it leads to the same predictable place: burnout for the coach, dependency for the client, and inconsistent results for everyone.

What client fulfillment really means is creating a full, end-to-end experience for your clients. This includes everything from how your product is structured, to how clearly you communicate, to those small, thoughtful touches that make clients feel valued. (But remember: Gestures like sending a handwritten note or gifting something meaningful at the right moment may be nice, little "wow" moments that stand out, but they aren't the foundation.)

The core of fulfillment is much simpler: Deliver exactly what you promised. Most businesses fail at this basic step, which means doing it well immediately sets you apart.

At Smart Mentoring, we've learned that successful delivery isn't about removing every obstacle from the client's path. Instead we focus on building systems that help them move through the obstacles. We can't prevent every challenge, but we can prepare both client success manager and client for when those challenges inevitably arise.

What follows are eight principles of scalable, client fulfillment. These practices allow you to deliver exceptional results without micromanaging, rescuing, or carrying your clients.

1. The "step ahead" principle and predictive support

When one of our clients launches their first premium-priced offer, their biggest challenges aren't usually technical, but emotional. They announce their $5,000 service publicly, and suddenly people start questioning their worth and they hear things like, "Who do you think you are?" and "Why would anyone pay that much?"

Unfortunately, no amount of mindset prep can fully prevent that emotional wave. Feelings like shame, fear, and self-doubt eventually come to the surface. What I want you to know is nothing is wrong with this. It's simply a natural response to stepping into a bigger identity. And just like a parent can't shield a child from every painful experience in life, a mentor can't (and shouldn't) protect clients from all discomfort. Our job is not to eliminate the fear but to equip clients to keep moving despite it.

That's why one of the most powerful things you can do as a mentor is not to shield clients from discomfort, but to prepare them for it. When you've guided dozens or even hundreds of people through the same transformation, you start to recognize the emotional patterns: the excitement at the beginning, the hesitation in week three, the resistance when something stretches their identity, the dip that happens right before the breakthrough.

You learn to map not only the high-high moments but also the predictable low-lows. And when you bring those to the surface in advance—"Here's what will likely happen next, and here's why it's normal"—you remove the element of surprise. The challenging moments no longer feel like personal failures to the client; they feel like part of the process.

This is what responsible delivery really looks like. Not carrying your clients through every difficult step, not rushing to rescue them, not rewriting their decisions to keep them comfortable—but equipping them to walk through the discomfort with clarity and strength.

When you do that, clients stay empowered, the relationship stays clean, and they build the resilience required for real transformation.

2. Setting expectations

When you first begin charging higher prices, it's easy to slip into over-delivery mode. You feel the weight of someone's investment, and without realizing it, you start trying to compensate with extra calls, extra access, or bending the boundaries of your offer. I did this myself in the beginning. I promised my first thirty clients a two-hour response time. It was completely unsustainable—and it didn't improve their results at all. When I later removed that promise, nothing changed except that clients became more resourceful and I became a better leader.

The real foundation of a high-ticket relationship is shared responsibility, and that begins with setting expectations clearly from the very beginning. Clients need to understand how the process works, what support they can rely on, what actions are required from them, and what success actually depends on. When expectations are clear, clients know what's theirs to own and what's yours to provide. If you offer done-for-you services, scope and timelines are defined upfront. If you coach or consult, you establish that your role is to provide the system, feedback, and structure, while their role is to implement, communicate, and take action consistently. This clarity prevents the subtle slide into emotional caretaking or over-responsibility.

The truth is, misunderstandings rarely happen because the strategy is unclear; they happen because expectations were never explicitly stated. By setting them early, you create a partnership where trust grows, boundaries hold, and both sides can do their best work without carrying what doesn't belong to them.

3. The paradox of responsibility

The paradox of responsibility in coaching is that true responsibility means refusing to take on what isn't yours. You can offer world-class systems, frameworks, support, foresight, and structure. You can prepare clients for what's coming, normalize the messy parts, and give them tools to move through fear. But you cannot take responsibility for whether someone shows up, follows through, or manages their emotions.

There is a lot you can (and really, must) do to help clients succeed. But there is also a boundary, and crossing it does more harm than good. When a coach over-functions, the client under-functions. When coaches take on too much responsibility, clients lose theirs. They stop owning their own transformation. They start outsourcing their decision-making, doubting themselves, or waiting for permission instead of trusting the process. And eventually, their results plateau.

The goal isn't to remove difficulty but to build a process that helps clients move through it. That's what real fulfillment systems are designed to do.

4. Client Health Score

To stay grounded in objectivity rather than emotion, our team uses something called the Client Health Score. It tracks both tangible progress and trust in the process. Clients who trust the process tend to implement consistently. If they fall behind, they communicate honestly and get back on track. Clients who lose trust begin to hesitate, reinvent their approach, or question the system.

The Client Health Score helps us identify these moments early. We use milestone tracking, behavioral patterns, and regular touchpoints to understand where each client is in their journey. When the score dips, it's not automatically a failure. It often indicates that the client is in the messy middle, which is the hardest part of any transformation. In those moments, we tighten communication, reaffirm the plan, and guide them back to the proven path, without abandoning the structure that works.

In other words, we manage *client state*, not client emotions. We don't guarantee that everything will feel easy. We guarantee that we will guide them through the hard parts without losing sight of the goal.

5. The *"karhunpalvelus"* effect

One of the biggest pitfalls in coaching is something Finns call *karhunpalvelus* (KAR-hoon-PAL-veh-loos)—a "bear's service." It's when you try to help someone but end up harming them. This happens when a coach gives in to a client's fear and allows them to steer the strategy away from the proven process. It often sounds like, "Can we test something different?" or "This post feels too scary to share" or "I think this method just doesn't work for my niche." These requests come from genuine fear and not strategy. If the coach follows them into unfamiliar territory, results drop and trust drops too. The client ends up believing their fear was right all along.

This is why structure protects both sides. In situations like this, we stay transparent: "You're welcome to test a different approach, but we can't promise the same results if we leave the proven path." This kind of honesty keeps expectations clear and preserves both authority and trust.

6. When clients don't get results

Even with a proven system, not every client hits their target. It happens. What matters is understanding *why*, because the reason almost always falls into one of two categories.

The first is a loss of trust in the process. When clients get scared, they start hesitating, second-guessing, or trying to reinvent the method altogether. They pull away from the structure that works and begin relying on instinct or emotion instead. When this happens, the solution is not to adjust the strategy to soothe the fear but rather to reaffirm the "why."

We explain why the process works, show examples and data, and bring the client back to the proven path. Trust is rebuilt through transparency and clarity, not apology.

The second reason is that their goal has genuinely changed. Sometimes, halfway through the program, clients realize they no longer want what they originally pursued. Their priorities shift. Their definition of success evolves. When this happens, the solution is a simple, human conversation: Redefine the target, clarify expectations, and decide on a new focus if needed.

If the issue is trust, we strengthen structure and communication. If the issue is a new goal, we revisit the vision. In both cases, honesty cures confusion.

What we *never* do is apologize for a client's lack of implementation. That muddies ownership and unintentionally reinforces the belief that results depend on the coach rather than the client. Instead, we hold space for emotion while keeping accountability intact.

7. Understanding the pace of progress

Results aren't always immediate or financial, and part of delivering at scale is recognizing that. Every client who truly implements—no matter how slowly—experiences breakthroughs in clarity, confidence, and mindset along the way.

As our operational director often says, "I've never seen a single client who implemented fully, communicated openly, and trusted the process who didn't get results, even if it took longer than expected."

That's the power of a strong fulfillment system: When clients follow the path and stay engaged, transformation stops being a question of *if* and becomes a matter of *when*.

8. Scaling the fulfillment machine

By now, you should understand that emotional management doesn't scale. What *does* scale, however, are systems. That's why we treat fulfillment like a transformation machine rather than a collection of individual client problems. A fulfillment machine is a set of repeatable processes that deliver consistent outcomes no matter how many clients you serve or how many emotional waves they experience along the way.

In practice, that means every client moves through the same set of standardized milestones, which makes their progress clear and measurable. Over time, we've seen the same emotional patterns repeat themselves, so we now plan our interventions before challenges appear. Our Client Health Score shows when trust or engagement begins to dip (often before the client even expresses it) so we can support them proactively. And because every client walks the same proven path, our authority strengthens through repetition; we can speak with certainty about what works, what doesn't, and why.

This structure is what allows Smart Mentoring to deliver consistent results across hundreds of clients without needing me on client calls.

The bottom line in all of this is that *growth is a partnership*. Scalable fulfillment only works when responsibility is shared. The client brings commitment, honest communication, and consistent implementation.

The coach brings structure, foresight, and accountability. Each side owns their 50 percent.

Filtering Clients

As you refine your delivery, you begin to see that fulfillment isn't only about supporting clients well. Perhaps just as important, it's also about supporting the *right* clients well. Even the best-designed system can only take someone as far as they're willing to go. After working with hundreds of entrepreneurs, one truth becomes impossible to ignore: Your client's behavior matters just as much as your curriculum.

When I first started my entrepreneurial journey, I avoided premium offers and focused on selling low-ticket, do-it-yourself courses. In hindsight, if I think about that deeply, that decision came from fear. Charging a few hundred dollars for a self-paced course felt safe. There was no real pressure. If someone didn't get results, it didn't feel connected to me.

But when you move into high-ticket programs, everything becomes more binding. The level of commitment rises on both sides. Clients invest more, so naturally their expectations grow and so does the pressure to deliver. At first, that can feel overwhelming. You want to give them everything, to prove their trust was worth it. You might even believe their success rests entirely on your shoulders.

Over time, though, you begin to see a pattern: Some clients follow the process and get incredible results, while others resist every step and blame you when things don't work out. The difference isn't the product. It's the client.

That's why filtering matters just as much as building your offer. If you accept everyone, you'll end up with clients who drain your energy, resist the process, or sabotage their own success. The real question is, "Which type of client will get results through this process?" Instead of trying to be a fit for the entire world, you get crystal clear on who your program is truly designed for *and* who it's not for.

Take two clients I worked with who coached highly educated women interested in starting side businesses. In the beginning, they enrolled anyone who was willing to pay. Over time, they started noticing consistent patterns:

- Clients who started with a very low upfront payment—under $1,000 on a $5,000 offer—almost always asked for refunds later.
- Clients chasing "passive income" without a concrete business idea rarely followed through on the work.
- The best results came from women who already had a clear business idea, were willing to commit at least ten hours per week, and made a serious initial investment.

Once these clients realized their messaging was attracting the wrong type of client, they refined how they spoke about their offer. They focused their marketing directly on the women who were already getting the best results—those who were decisive, committed, and ready to take action. This adjustment in messaging naturally filtered out clients who weren't a fit. As a result, their energy improved, their clients' results strengthened, and referrals increased. Refunds and complaints decreased dramatically, because they were now working with people who fully understood the process and were willing to follow it. By narrowing their focus, they elevated the experience and outcomes for every client they served.

Now, you might not know these types of patterns at the beginning. This is another reason why beta groups are so valuable. With a larger group of initial clients, you see diverse behaviors play out in real time. You get to test your process across different personalities and industries. Over time, you'll develop a clear picture of exactly who thrives in your program and who doesn't.

From there, you can stop saying yes to everyone and start saying yes to the right people.

Ethical Scaling Systems

One of the most powerful lessons I've learned about scaling isn't just about systems for delivery—it's about systems for capturing and amplifying success.

What does that mean? It means we don't just wait around for clients to share their wins. Instead, we've built a process that makes celebrating results a natural part of the journey. With the help of Jay Goncalves and Adam Molloy from Ethical Scaling, we created a framework where client milestones automatically trigger the next step.

For example:

- When a client hits a major milestone, our client success manager immediately asks for a referral.
- If the client doesn't have someone to refer, we pivot and ask them for a testimonial instead.
- Later, when they've seen consistent results, we introduce the next-level offer (the "backend offer").

This approach ensures that success stories don't slip through the cracks. Our client success managers even have KPIs tied to client wins. That means they actively check in—"How did this week go? Do you have any wins or positive focus you'd like to share?"—so that progress gets celebrated and captured.

The key here is nothing passive. We don't wait for testimonials, referrals, or case studies to magically appear. We've systematized it so that client wins become a predictable part of our growth engine. At one point, I even asked our Facebook community to drop their wins in the comments of a post, and dozens poured in. That single thread became a goldmine of social proof.

Ethical scaling isn't about squeezing clients for more; it's about building fair, repeatable systems that celebrate success, amplify results, and allow you to grow without compromising the client experience.

At Smart Mentoring, we've invested heavily to make our delivery as seamless and scalable as possible. We've refined our curriculum, hired consultants, and built a playbook for our client success team. Today, our front-end program runs smoothly without me having to personally deliver it. I can trust that clients are well-supported because the systems are strong.

The structure of our program also helps with scalability. All of our clients start from a similar place (because we filter for that) and move toward a similar outcome. This eliminates the need for heavy customization and makes it easier to deliver consistent results at scale.

Expansion Through Backend Offers

Something I learned from Jay Goncalves from Ethical Scaling was that scaling does not come from adding more complexity, more products, or more team members. Real scaling happens when you increase output with the same input—when revenue, retention, and client results grow without the operational load growing with them.

This is where backend offers come in.

Most founders think of their Client Success (CS) team as a cost center—"the people who support clients after they buy." But when built the right way, your CS team becomes a self-liquidating team, meaning they pay for themselves many times over. In addition to delivering support, their role is to generate backend revenue, renewals, and referrals by helping clients stay longer, succeed more, and ascend further into your ecosystem.

That's why in our company, the CS team carries KPIs just like the sales team. They're measured on retention, renewals, referrals, and backend sales (upsells or continuation offers). They are measured not only by how well clients perform, but also by how many clients continue in our ecosystem.

The key is designing backend offers that meet clients exactly where they are. Not every client finishes at the same stage, and backend offers should reflect that. For example:

- **Clients who achieved strong results:** These are perfect fits for a more advanced mastermind or leadership-level container—something that gives them community, higher-level strategy, events, or support with team building, scaling, or personal branding.
- **Clients who did "okay":** These clients need a continuation or optimization program—something focused on consistency, refining their systems, and solidifying what they've already built.

- **Clients who struggled or got partially stuck:** These clients often need deeper support, not less. This "deeper support" track is designed to help them finally achieve the breakthrough they've been working toward.

When you look at retention as a service, you're not just selling "more time"; you're providing the next level of support based on the client's journey. The goal is to create the *next logical step* for each client—support that actually fits their stage and gives them the best chance of reaching the results they came for.

One more important insight: Founders often assume that clients who didn't get the best results "can't afford to continue." In reality, many of them *can* and *will* continue when the next step is clearly positioned as the support they've been missing. They're often the people who need the backend offer the most.

Pro Tip: Turn Client Goodwill into Referrals

One of the most cost-efficient and scalable ways to grow your business is through referrals. When clients feel supported, seen, and successful, they build what I call a goodwill bank account. Asking for a referral then becomes natural, not awkward. The secret is timing. Ask when they're already feeling a win.

The best moments to ask for referrals:

- Right after onboarding (excitement is high)
- After a mindset or confidence breakthrough
- When they land a new client or hit a milestone
- When they finish a major module or submit a key deliverable

At Smart Mentoring, we've taken this further and systemized it through something we call the Celebration Call. Whenever a client hits a milestone, our Client Success Manager immediately books a call to celebrate with them. On this call, we give them a small gift (a restaurant gift card, for example) and ask them to share how they went from where they started to the results they're now experiencing. If they're open to it, that call becomes a natural moment to capture a testimonial *and* ask if they know anyone who might be a fit for the program.

When a client is proud, excited, and feeling momentum, they are in the ideal mindset to share their story and refer others. Ask too early or too late, and you miss the window.

When the moment is right, use a simple, conversational script: "Hey, now that you've signed your first client, do you happen to know another coach who's serious about growing their business with premium offers and could benefit from our help?"

If they respond with something like, "Hmm, I don't think so…," you can gently follow up by asking, "You've been happy working with us, right?" Once they confirm, you simply say, "Perfect. Would it be okay if I send you a short message you can forward to anyone who comes to mind later?"

Asking for permission rather than asking for names removes all pressure, and providing a ready-made message does the heavy lifting for them. This tiny system turns client goodwill into ongoing organic growth—effortlessly and ethically.

Key Takeaways

#1. Your product is your reputation.
A high-ticket product isn't defined by price but by its ability to deliver a clear, repeatable transformation at scale. When the outcome, milestones, and delivery systems are well-designed, your product becomes the foundation of your business.

#2. Structure beats customization.
Scalable client delivery comes from clear expectations, boundaries, predictive support (being one step ahead), and tools like Client Health Scores—not from rescuing, over-functioning, or carrying your clients' emotions.

#3. **Fulfillment is systems, not emotional management.**
Results happen in partnership. Your role is to provide a proven process, tools, and support. Your clients' role is to show up and take action. Clear expectations protect both sides, prevent burnout, and empower clients to take ownership of their transformation.

#4. **The right clients are as important as the right product.**
Filtering for readiness, commitment, and fit is non-negotiable. When you choose clients who are willing to implement and take responsibility, results improve, refunds drop, energy rises, and your whole ecosystem becomes easier to run.

#5. **Ethical scaling amplifies success; it doesn't squeeze it.**
Systems for referrals, testimonials, backend offers, and tailored continuation paths turn client wins into organic growth. Your client success team becomes a revenue and retention engine, and growth happens by serving existing clients better, not by endlessly adding more.

Strategies & Tools

Now that you've seen the philosophy and structure behind building a high-ticket product, this section gives you the practical tools to bring it to life. These three strategies—building the product, supporting clients at scale, and turning results into a growth engine—work together to create a program that is predictable, high-touch, and scalable.

What follows are the exact processes you can use to deliver consistent transformation, support more clients without burning out, and leverage your client results to attract the next wave of buyers.

How to Build a High-Ticket Product

We covered these concepts throughout the chapter, but sometimes you need everything in one place. What follows is a simple, step-by-step guide you can use to structure, validate, and refine your high-ticket product.

1. **Start with the outcome.** Define one clear, measurable transformation. Reverse-engineer your ideal client based on who is most likely to achieve it.
2. **Create milestones.** Break the transformation into five to twelve milestones, and for each one clarify what the client must learn, what action they must take, and what counts as proof of completion—giving only the minimum information needed for the next step and not allowing clients to move forward until the current milestone is complete.
3. **Choose simple delivery.** Use the lightest possible setup: weekly calls, Google Drive/Notion curriculum, Slack/WhatsApp support, and weekly check-ins. Start live, then record and systemize once refined.
4. **Validate with a paid pilot.** Run a small, paid pilot (five to ten ideal clients) at a reduced rate. Deliver live, gather feedback, refine weekly, and collect testimonials and data. This is your proof of demand.
5. **Build fulfillment systems.** Map the entire client journey: onboarding, first action, check-ins, communication boundaries, feedback loops, and offboarding. Make it simple, personal, and repeatable.
6. **Refine with data.** Track where clients get stuck, what produces results, and what questions repeat. Document processes, build FAQ libraries, and use a Client Health Score to maintain consistency. Raise your price once results are predictable.

When you build your product this way—outcome-first, milestone-driven, validated in the real world, and supported by intentional systems—you stop relying on luck and start relying on structure.

Scalable Client Support Systems

Once your product is structured and your fulfillment systems are in place, the next layer is how you support clients day-to-day. High-ticket clients expect access, responsiveness, and personalized attention—but emotional management doesn't scale, so your support channels need to be intentionally designed.

Today, my team includes two full-time client success managers whose sole focus is client results. With the right systems, one manager can support up to fifty clients at a time—sometimes more, depending on the structure of your offer. Ethical Scaling consultants Jay Goncalves and Ben McLellan have seen that number go as high as seventy-five per manager. For us, fifty feels good since we still include one-on-one calls alongside group coaching.

The key is to design communication that feels high-touch while remaining scalable. Here's the structure we use:

- **Slack for day-to-day support.** Clients can reach out anytime in dedicated private Slack channels, allowing us to respond quickly without needing to schedule dozens of calls. It keeps support accessible while preserving your calendar.
- **Short calls reserved for deeper work.** If something requires a more nuanced conversation, we book a focused twenty- to thirty-minute call. This keeps capacity predictable while ensuring clients get personalized attention exactly when they need it.
- **Voice notes and video messages for connection.** A quick voice note or video often provides the same emotional reassurance as a live call without the time drain. These small touches maintain intimacy while keeping delivery lean.

This blend of structured systems and personal communication creates a support experience that feels high-touch without overwhelming you or your team. Clients feel seen, supported, and guided, while you maintain the capacity to scale. And when you offer this level of thoughtful, private support—whether through messaging access, one-on-one calls, or a dedicated client hub—you can confidently sell higher-touch consulting products.

Treat Results Like an Asset

Client results are the most powerful driver of organic growth. Every success story becomes marketing for the next client. Those results can fuel your entire marketing engine through content, case studies, and testimonials that naturally bring in the next wave of clients.

This is exactly how I grew my business in the early years without spending a single dollar on ads. Consistency and client results fueled organic growth. Even now, as we experiment with paid ads, so many of our clients still come directly from organic content. Someone recently booked after telling me he'd been silently following my posts on LinkedIn for months before finally reaching out.

The key to making this sustainable is to *treat results like an asset.* Build a system around collecting and sharing them so that it happens automatically, not as an afterthought.

Here's what that looks like in our business:

- **Document every client win.** Whenever a client shares a success—big or small—our team logs it in Slack.
- **Feed it directly into marketing.** Our marketing team takes those wins and turns them into social posts, email content, webinar stories, or YouTube case studies.
- **Get permissions upfront.** In our client agreements, we include a clause that allows us to use first names and results for marketing purposes. This way, we're never chasing down approval later.
- **Repurpose in multiple formats.** If a client doesn't have time for a full interview, I take their story and write it up as a case study, then film a short video sharing their success. More than once, clients have been blown away seeing their own progress laid out in writing.

We then use these stories everywhere—emails, posts, videos, even as examples in sales conversations. Each one builds trust and reinforces the message: *This process works.*

When you make client success part of your system from day one, it compounds over time. Dozens of real stories and testimonials create a reputation that sells for you. People are able to see undeniable proof of transformation.

Final Thoughts

Your product is the heartbeat of your business—the place where transformation happens and where your reputation is truly built. When a client enters a well-designed program, one with clear milestones, intentional delivery, and supportive systems, their progress becomes predictable rather than accidental. You stop relying on inspiration, improvisation, or "hoping it works," and begin operating from structure and consistency.

This chapter laid out the foundations of that structure: starting with a clear outcome, breaking it into milestones, validating your process through real clients, supporting them with scalable communication systems, and filtering for the people who are most likely to succeed. When these pieces are in place, client results compound. Every win strengthens your product, sharpens your process, and reinforces your confidence as the creator of a method that genuinely works.

Treating results as an asset—and building systems to capture, celebrate, and learn from them—allows your product to evolve continuously. Instead of reinventing the wheel, you refine what's already delivering outcomes. Instead of absorbing responsibility for every struggle, you work with clients who are ready to meet you halfway. And instead of stretching yourself thinner as you grow, your systems hold the weight so you don't have to.

This is how a high-ticket product becomes scalable. Not through complexity, but through clarity, boundaries, and repeatability. And as soon as your product becomes reliable at scale, you unlock something even more important: the ability to lead your business, rather than be consumed by it.

In the next chapter, we'll explore what happens when you move from being a scrappy solopreneur to leading a business that's bigger than you—and why growth, while exciting, can also be one of the hardest transitions you'll ever make.

CHAPTER 4

THE SOLOPRENEUR TRAP AND THE PAIN OF SCALING

"If you got hit by a bus, would your company survive?"

That was a question one of my mentors asked me. At the time, my entire business revolved around me—my energy, my decisions, my ability to juggle everything at once. Deep down, I knew the honest answer: No, it wouldn't survive. And that was a problem.

Scaling sounds glamorous from the outside: bigger numbers, bigger launches, bigger milestones. But behind the scenes, I felt the weight of it every day. Sleepless nights, constant decision-making, the anxiety of leading people when I wasn't sure of my own footing. I remember waking up with my chest tight, like I was about to step onto a stage, except the performance never ended. Growth wasn't just exciting, it was exhausting.

Growth also exposes the cracks—delegation fears, "I can fix this" thinking, overcomplicating everything—and without the right systems in place, those cracks widen fast. Over time, I started to notice that many of my clients were struggling with what I call solopreneur traps. Things like carrying too much of their business alone, fearing delegation, and trying to scale without structure. Even if I hadn't fallen into those traps myself, I could see how easy it was to get stuck in them. And as my own business grew, I understood just how fragile things can become when too much depends on one person.

This chapter is about those solopreneur traps: the hidden mindsets and mistakes that make scaling painful, and the turning points that taught me how to build a business designed to last—whether I was in the room or not.

The Pain of Scaling

Building a team was always part of my vision. By the time 2022 came around and I had finally reached my breakthrough product, I was already thinking ahead—how could I scale? How could I build a team, but this time, do it better?

This wasn't my first time hiring. When I was selling podcast services during my Career Girl days, I had assembled a small commission-based sales team. But looking back, that wasn't really organized—it was testing. We didn't have a product-market fit back then. We were experimenting, trying to make something work. We got a few sales here and there, but it wasn't sustainable. The demand wasn't there.

Determined to do it better this time, I did what I always do: dove into books, podcasts, and mentors for advice. I'd spent months reading books, listening to podcasts, and researching how to find an "operator" or hire an operations manager. The advice sounded perfect in theory—bring in someone to run the show so I could focus on my zone of genius, that unique area where my skills and passion line up to produce the best results.

So, I posted a job ad, interviewed one person, and hired her.

She wasn't a stranger; we had met through my common networks. She told me she loved what I was building and she wanted to be part of it. She believed in me. That kind of enthusiasm was hard to ignore, especially when you're building something personal and ambitious. I was excited—she believed in what I was doing, and she was eager to contribute. She encouraged me to return to serving entrepreneurs after a brief detour into B2B. On the surface, it seemed like the perfect fit.

And at first, it really did feel that way. I was relieved to finally have help and confident she could take some pressure off. But as we started working together, small cracks began to appear. I had more experience than she did, and that quickly started to show. There was a clear mismatch in how we worked, in our pace, and in our standards. I had that gut feeling early on, but I brushed it off. I didn't fully trust my instincts, and I didn't know what a "good hire" felt like yet.

Mentors and other entrepreneurs kept telling me, "You have to train your team. No one comes in knowing everything." It made sense in theory, but I didn't have training materials. No real onboarding process. I certainly didn't have any systems in place. I didn't understand what kind of person this role required. I just handed her tasks and hoped she would figure them out.

One of her first responsibilities was to help with hiring. And she did—fast. Within a few months, we went from just me to a team of more than ten people. She was writing job ads, running interviews, and onboarding new team members. I was still looped in, but barely. It felt like I was showing up to a new company every week—new faces, new roles, and my own responsibilities constantly shifting.

I couldn't keep up. It was as if I had lost all control. I was overwhelmed by the constant changes. I didn't recognize the business anymore. I had started it, nurtured it, and watched it grow, but now it felt like I was just a passenger. The constant rotation of people, the shifting roles—it all felt chaotic and out of my hands. Even the team culture had changed. It no longer reflected the way I used to work. I found myself getting frustrated by small things, annoyed by how the team operated, and disconnected from the kind of culture I wanted to build. It wasn't just the lack of stability—it was the sense that I wasn't in charge anymore. I couldn't even get a clear grasp on what was happening from day to day. Everything was slipping through my fingers.

I wasn't sleeping. I was anxious all the time. It felt like I was building a house on sand.

Eventually, I had to face the truth: This wasn't working.

Admitting that was painful. In Finland, employees begin with a trial period, usually lasting between three and six months. I opted for the full six months for my first operations hire, knowing that either party could walk away without explanation during that time. After those six months, it becomes far more complex and costly for the employer if the employment needs to end.

Over the next six months, I tried to make it work. The truth, though, was that I had hired someone who wasn't suited for an operations role, and I was trying to mold her into something she wasn't. She had never been an operations manager before—either in my industry or elsewhere. I didn't set clear expectations, and while we had KPIs, they weren't met. I didn't hold her accountable, partly because I wasn't fully confident in how to manage her, and partly because of my people-pleasing tendencies. I struggled to enforce high standards without feeling like I was hurting someone's feelings.

She was also the type of person who said yes to everything. At first, that seemed positive, but when you're a visionary with dozens of new ideas each week, what you need is someone who challenges you. Someone who can push back and say, "This isn't working with our current strategy," or "We don't have the capacity for this right now." Instead, everything I suggested was met with enthusiastic agreement. That resulted in a business that kept shifting directions without a strong strategy to guide us. We constantly tried new things, hoping they would work, but that kind of experimentation requires time—three to six months to see if a new direction even has traction. We were burning energy and delaying results.

Eventually, after the trial period ended, I tried to shift her role. I suggested narrowing her focus to a specific department or smaller piece of the business. But by that point, we were too misaligned. I had figured out a product-market fit, but I hadn't built the systems and processes to allow someone else to step in and manage the business. She wasn't equipped to build those systems either, and I didn't know how to lead her through it. So internally, we floundered.

What made it even more confusing was that during those early months, revenue was strong. It looked like we were growing. It felt like the right time to scale. We were still getting clients and never had a zero-sales month. In fact, the summer of 2022 brought in some of our best revenue.

That didn't last long, though. By early 2023, revenue had significantly decreased.

I had tried to build for continued growth—more people, more infrastructure—assuming the revenue would keep climbing. When it didn't, I found myself with a bloated team and shrinking margins.

A mentor told me the problem was clear: I was heading in one direction, while the team—especially the operations manager—was heading in another. His comment solidified what I already knew.

I had to make a change.

Hard Truths

One of the reasons I had wanted an operations manager was so I wouldn't have to have hard conversations. She took on the responsibility of hiring, managing, and firing team members, allowing me to stay removed from the uncomfortable aspects of leadership. But by avoiding discomfort, I only delayed the inevitable. Entrepreneurship forces you to confront the very things you're trying to avoid. You can't outsource hard conversations forever. As Alex Hormozi says, "The life you want is on the other side of a few hard conversations."

When I finally let her go, I actually felt lighter—more in control than I had in months. I took full leadership of the company again. The situation with clients had already stabilized, and I was ready to rebuild the internal structure properly this time.

That period was intense. I was still dealing with sleepless nights, managing team transitions, and leading through uncertainty. It was not easy. I had to have hard conversations, fire people who weren't a fit, and recruit new team members with higher standards. Each conversation weighed on me, but I knew this was necessary to build the kind of company I wanted to lead.

One of my friends, who later became my leadership coach, told me: "You're like a wartime CEO." And it really did feel like that—steadying the ship while everything around me demanded quick, high-stakes decisions.

The business wasn't failing. We brought in around $760,000 that year, which was objectively strong. But behind the scenes, it felt like everything was breaking at once. Scaling before we were truly ready didn't just cost money; it cost clarity, confidence, and peace of mind. It affected the team dynamic, the client experience, and my own ability to lead from a calm place. And while we didn't crash, we did overextend. I had learned how fragile a business becomes when you scale without infrastructure. I had also learned how expensive—emotionally and financially—a wrong hire can be.

And, most importantly, I had learned that delegation without systems isn't delegation.

It's chaos.

Solopreneur Traps

More than just strategy or numbers, scaling is about the mindset shifts that allow you to stop carrying the whole business on your back. In the early days, most of us operate like solopreneurs—hustling, wearing every hat, and convincing ourselves it's the only way. That season can teach you resilience, but it can also trap you.

Solopreneur traps are patterns of thinking and behaving that feel safe in the moment but quietly keep you stuck. They show up as resistance to delegation, clinging to people who aren't working out, or overcomplicating your business until you don't even recognize what you're building. I've lived all of these traps. I convinced myself I was the only one clients wanted. I tried to fix people who weren't right for the job. I added layer after layer of complexity until the business was bloated and fragile.

When you want to scale, these traps are as frustrating as they are dangerous. They drain your energy, blur your focus, and make growth feel harder than it needs to be. The good news is, once you see them, you can start to step out of them.

Trap 1: The Delegation Myth

In my early years, delegation wasn't something I resisted—it was something I intentionally built toward. I never saw myself as just a coach or service provider; I saw myself as a business builder. From the beginning,

I wanted to create a company that didn't rely entirely on me. So when I hired my first operations manager, it wasn't necessarily because I was afraid to delegate; it was because I thought that's what a growing business was supposed to do. My mentors and coaches encouraged it, and I followed the playbook.

What I didn't realize at the time, though, was that *how* you delegate matters just as much as *who* you hire. I thought I needed senior-level people with big titles—people who could manage and strategize. But what I actually needed was support in the day-to-day execution.

That belief showed up in small ways. I avoided using the word *assistant* because it didn't sound strategic enough. At one point, I called someone a "sales coordinator" instead. Looking back now, I can see I was trying to project a level of sophistication the business wasn't ready for yet.

I quickly changed my perspective when I was in a coworking space in Portugal, sitting beside a friend who also ran a business. She asked casually, "Don't you have an assistant?" When I said no, she looked surprised. She didn't even have kids, and yet she had two assistants—one for her personal life and one for her business.

To her, it was obvious. To me, it was revelatory. Maybe it didn't have to be so hard.

That summer, I finally hired my first executive assistant, Mia. She wasn't there to manage or strategize; she was there to make my life easier. And she did. Mia loved the things I hated: spreadsheets, reports, color-coded Excel files (she even made them for her holidays). For the first time, I saw that there are people who thrive in the tasks I resist.

Not long after came Saana, who would redefine what I thought a team member could be. She joined as a client success manager and, within months, was building entire course materials on her own. She didn't crumble under feedback; she absorbed it and improved. One night, she was still at my home office while I was already eating dinner in the next room with my family, long after I'd finished work, determined to complete a project. That kind of drive isn't teachable.

Mia and Saana showed me what was possible in people. They proved delegation wasn't a burden—it was liberation. And once I experienced that, my standards changed. I stopped shrinking my vision out of fear and started dreaming bigger again.

Trap 2: The "I Can Fix This" Mentality

There's a unique kind of exhaustion that comes from carrying the wrong person on your team. I know because I did it for far too long.

In the first year of serious scaling, my team ballooned with salespeople, marketers, operations. On paper, everything was covered. But I felt out of control in my own company, and things still weren't moving in the right direction. Deep down, I knew one of the hires wasn't right. I didn't trust them, but instead of making the hard call, I convinced myself: "Maybe I can fix this."

That mentality was so wrong. I would wake up each morning feeling like I was at the starting line of a race I hadn't trained for. Adrenaline and anxiety coursed through me for weeks. My nervous system was fried. And still, I told myself one more try might change things.

It never did.

The truth was, I had outsourced responsibility without creating structure. I thought hiring someone meant they would figure things out for me. I kept handing them the wheel, only to feel more and more lost in my own business. That's the worst feeling, when you can't even name your role anymore, because you've given away both the clarity and the control.

Looking back, that season taught me a painful but necessary truth: You can't "fix" the wrong hire. Wishing and waiting only magnifies the dysfunction. And while letting someone go can feel like ripping a seam, keeping them on too long tears the whole fabric.

It was one of the hardest cycles I've lived through as a leader. But it also forced me to confront the way I avoided decisions under the guise of optimism. Telling myself "maybe I can fix this" was really just me avoiding hard conversations.

Trap 3: Overcomplicating Everything

When growth first came, I thought the answer was more—more channels, more strategies, more layers of marketing. If something wasn't working, my instinct was to add another campaign or experiment instead of simply improving what already existed. Soon, the business was bloated. We had marketing efforts running in multiple countries, new experiments every month, and no clear throughline.

The turning point came during my second pregnancy. The pressure of knowing I'd need time away forced me to face reality: The business wasn't stable. It couldn't run without me. And that's when I made the hardest—and smartest—choice: It was time to simplify!

We pulled back from international expansion and focused solely on Finland. We translated everything into one language. We stopped layering in experiments and went back to what had worked from the beginning. For the first time in months, things felt clear.

Looking back, I've realized that breakthroughs rarely come from doing more. They come from letting go:

1. Letting go of multiple offers and focusing on one
2. Letting go of the tasks on your plate and delegating them to others
3. Letting go of problems by simply solving them—without overthinking

And in that order. Stop overcomplicating things, and start letting them go.

Trap 4: Overlooking Hidden Strengths

For a long time, I believed no one would ever want to do the mundane, "boring" work—the inbox management, calendar coordination, data tracking, and process documentation that drained me. I assumed those tasks were burdensome and that asking someone to take them on would be selfish.

But guess what? Some people absolutely thrive in exactly those roles.

When I finally hired Mia, my first executive assistant, she relieved me from this trap. She lit up doing the very things I dreaded—spreadsheets, organization, detailed reporting. What felt heavy to me was energizing to her. Watching her in her element was a revelation.

The trap wasn't just my reluctance to delegate—it was my narrow view of what people might find fulfilling. By embracing the idea that different personalities are wired for different kinds of work, I opened the door to attracting true A-players. These were the people who didn't just lighten my load; they elevated the entire business. And they let me be in my zone of genius.

Trap 5: Building Your Business on Trainees

One of my mentors once said something that stuck with me: "Tesla wasn't built with trainees."

In the early days, I thought I was being smart by saving money on hires. I wasn't intentionally hiring underqualified people—I simply didn't yet understand how important recruiting truly was. I often hired the first person I interviewed instead of taking the time to find the best fit for the role. Some of those hires had great potential, and a few even grew into incredible team members later on. But at the time, I didn't know what "great" looked like yet.

What I've learned since then is that oftentimes you need to experience—even by accident—what it's like to have a true rock star on your team. That one person shows you what's possible when delegation works the way it should. Suddenly, you can see the contrast between managing people who need direction and leading people who create direction.

But when your team is made up of trainees, you're not leading. Unfortunately, you're babysitting.

Instead of being free to focus on growth and vision, I was trapped in constant oversight. I spent my days fixing mistakes, answering questions, and micromanaging every detail. When things went wrong, I lost time *and* confidence. I started questioning my own leadership abilities, wondering if I was the problem.

Eventually, I realized the issue wasn't just in my leadership. It was who I had chosen to put on the bus. Underqualified hires aren't cheaper in the long run. In fact, they are expensive! They cost you clarity, progress, and peace of mind.

A lot of our clients fear that hiring a team will cost them freedom and energy. It's a common fear, and understandable—especially if your early experiences with hiring weren't great. But when it's done right, it's the opposite. The right people *give* you freedom and energy, because they take ownership of the very things that you don't want to be doing.

Now, when I hire, I look for people who can *move the business forward without me hovering*. People who bring new ideas and skills to the table, not just enthusiasm. Because you can't scale on potential alone. You scale on competence, ownership, and zone of genius (more on this in chapter 9).

Builders vs. Service Providers

There are two main types of experts I often see: the builder and the service provider.

The builder is the visionary—someone who loves developing ideas and architecting growth. Builders think in frameworks and leverage from the start. They're naturally drawn to strategy, structure, and optimization.

The service provider (or "doer") thrives in hands-on work, serving clients directly, and getting energy from that connection and impact. They find deep satisfaction in the delivery itself, not necessarily in building the systems that support it.

Neither one is better than the other. But knowing which one you are changes how you should scale your business.

If you're a builder, you'll need strong executors—people who can deliver the work with excellence so you can stay in your zone of strategy and vision. If you're a service provider, you'll need a builder beside you—someone who can design the systems, processes, and structure that allow your work to grow without relying on you for everything.

The friction begins when you try to build your business like the opposite type. Service providers who love delivery often struggle to step back from client work long enough to scale. Builders who resist structure end up surrounded by ideas without execution.

Self-awareness here saves years of frustration. You don't need to change who you are; you just need to hire your opposite. The right partnership between a builder and a doer is what turns a business from busy to scalable.

Leadership Standards That Make Scaling Possible

In the fall of 2025, after leading a series of quarterly meetings with my long-term clients, I began noticing the same themes repeating across every conversation. Busyness. Too many priorities. Prices too low. The wrong people in the wrong seats. Problems that had been circling for months—or even years.

What separates those who keep spinning from those who scale sustainably are higher standards. The entrepreneurs who move forward aren't necessarily the most talented or the most strategic. They've simply learned where to draw the line—what they will and won't tolerate, what matters most, and what needs to be let go. The following represent some basic standards that determine whether your company can actually scale. These were the things I wanted to say to each of my clients directly—brutally but with love.

Because if these issues stay unresolved, the business won't grow. It will stall.

Solve One Problem at a Time

Business is never free of problems. The moment you solve one, another appears—just at a higher level. In the early days, you worry about finding clients or covering expenses. Later, it's about managing people, contracts, or systems. The problems don't go away; they evolve with you.

I see this all the time with clients who feel frustrated that things still feel hard even after they've grown. But that's exactly how it's supposed to be. The quality of your problems is a reflection of your progress.

What matters isn't how many issues you can juggle—it's your ability to identify the most important one and solve it fully before moving on. Every breakthrough simply earns you the right to face better problems next. That's the real sign of growth.

You Get What You Tolerate

Your company's level isn't determined by your goals—it's determined by what you're willing to tolerate. You don't rise to your highest goals; you sink to your lowest standards.

If you accept clients who underpay, you'll have plenty of them. If you overlook mediocre work, it quietly becomes the norm. Your standards—not your dreams—set the true baseline of your business.

I learned this lesson the hard way. Early on, I kept a team member in a key role long after I knew they weren't the right fit. I told myself I could fix it—that with more guidance, more patience, more time, it would turn around. It never did. What I didn't realize then was that every time I tolerated what wasn't working, I was teaching the entire company what was acceptable.

It's easy to rationalize these things when growth is steady. You think, *It's fine for now. It'll get better.* But the cracks you ignore in good times become fractures in hard ones. Eventually, I had to face that my problem wasn't one person—it was my standards.

Business Interest Before Individual Interest

One of the hardest lessons I've had to learn as a leader is that a company isn't a family—it's a living system with a mission. Its job isn't to fulfill every individual preference but to move toward its goals. When that order flips—when decisions are made for comfort instead of clarity—everyone eventually pays the price.

In my early leadership years, I confused generosity with good leadership. I wanted my team to feel supported, appreciated, and trusted. If someone didn't want to take on a certain task, I'd let them skip it. If someone asked for a raise, I'd approve it quickly, even when the numbers didn't justify it. It came from a good place—but a company built on people-pleasing doesn't stay strong for long.

When growth slowed and pressure increased, I saw the consequences clearly. The business couldn't sustain the choices I had made from empathy instead of structure. As soon as a tougher period came, I realized I was the one left without a salary—and the company suffered. I had unintentionally made decisions that served individuals more than the business itself.

Putting the business first doesn't mean treating people coldly—it means protecting the structure that gives everyone stability. It means creating a culture where high standards, clarity, and accountability are acts of care. When the company thrives, everyone benefits.

The Team's Job Is to Make Your Life Easier

One of the most important leadership lessons I've learned is that your team's role isn't to fulfill their own career goals—it's to make the business stronger and your life easier. If their work adds stress instead of removing it, something's off—either it's the wrong person or the wrong role.

Many entrepreneurs flip that dynamic. They try to create a dream workplace for everyone else while quietly burning themselves out in the process. But if the company isn't healthy, no one wins. The business exists to grow, create impact, and give the founder the freedom to lead from clarity—not exhaustion. When every team member's work supports that, everyone benefits: The company becomes more stable, clients get better results, and the whole team gains long-term security.

I've learned this the hard way. Every time there's been the wrong person in the wrong role, it's shown up in my sleep and energy. I could feel it before I could name it—something wasn't working. And every time I've made the difficult decision to make a change, life has immediately become lighter and business has moved faster.

One of my founder friends put it best: "A team member's most important job is to make the leader's life easier." In hiring, I look for that mindset. If a candidate only talks about what they want to learn or achieve for themselves, it's usually a red flag. The best people say something different: "I want to help you, free your time, and make things run better."

Those are the ones who make scaling possible.

Piia's Story: From Jack-of-All-Trades to Agency Leader

When Piia first came into Smart Mentoring, she was the definition of a "jack-of-all-trades." Her marketing and branding agency looked like a *sekatavarakauppa*—a mixed store of tiny tasks, random projects, and low-ticket client work. Every day was packed, every hour filled, yet nothing she did felt like real progress. She was constantly working overtime, delivering at a high level, but stuck in a cycle where the effort she put in never matched the income she earned.

Her breaking point came the moment she realized she wanted to scale but physically couldn't. She had no hours left to sell. The hourly model boxed her in, and no matter how hard she worked, she could never get ahead. That's when she started to understand that you cannot scale a business that depends entirely on your effort.

The shift began when she learned to price based on value, not hours. In her creative field, billing hourly was the norm—almost unquestioned. Letting go of that mindset felt almost rebellious at first. But when she finally understood that clients care about outcomes, not minutes on a clock, everything changed. She stopped positioning herself as the "affordable freelancer" and stepped into the role of a strategic partner. That one shift opened the door to bigger clients, bigger projects, and bigger thinking.

At the beginning, Piia did everything herself. Sales, delivery, admin, design, communication—you name it, she did it. But as she raised her prices and her demand increased, she realized she had to shift from doing the work to leading the work. Today, she no longer handles most of the operational project execution at all. Her team does—and, as she often says with a laugh, "honestly, they do it better than I ever did."

Letting go wasn't easy. She had to learn to trust people, to stop micromanaging, and to give responsibility instead of tasks. With the right hires and the right project management tools, she began to see that leadership wasn't about control—it was about clarity. As soon as she built clear processes, her team could follow them, own them, and even improve them. That's when her business started to scale.

The journey wasn't without challenges. Hiring mistakes were painful and expensive—costing money, time, and emotional energy. She learned the hard way that the wrong hire can slow the entire company down. But she also learned that the right hire can accelerate everything. She experienced firsthand what this chapter teaches: A business scales through people, not the founder's personal hustle.

Another ongoing challenge was balancing sales and capacity. Some seasons brought more work than her team could deliver; other seasons were quieter. But even that taught her something essential: Scaling isn't a straight line—it's an ongoing practice of adjusting systems, refining processes, and strengthening leadership.

As her systems grew stronger, Piia's thinking expanded. Suddenly, €1 million in annual revenue didn't feel impossible—it felt inevitable. And that shift came not from flashy tactics, but from structure: weekly team check-ins, documented client processes, a project management system everyone followed, and a clearer understanding of what excellence looked like at every step. As she says, "As soon as I create a clear process, it's easier for others to follow and own it. That's how we scale."

Sales and marketing transformed too. In the early days, she waited for clients to find her. Now she creates content, reaches out proactively, and uses LinkedIn to build visibility and book calls. What gave her confidence wasn't personality—it was having a system. With a clear sales process and lead generation system, she no longer had to "wing it." She simply showed up and followed the structure.

Throughout her journey, Piia has often felt like an outsider—someone who never quite fit the mold in school, in traditional jobs, or even in early entrepreneurship. But what once felt like a disadvantage has become her superpower. She doesn't blend in; she stands out. Her agency doesn't look like everyone else's—and that difference is exactly why clients notice her. She shows up fully as herself, colorful clothes and all, and that authenticity has become a cornerstone of her authority.

The real validation, however, has come from client results. One client's brand transformation led to ongoing collaboration, increased visibility, and consistent lead flow. Almost every client she has worked with has experienced measurable growth. Those wins reminded her why she built her business in the first place—to create work that has real impact.

Now she's exploring new opportunities like fractional CMO roles, an area barely tapped in Finland. Abroad, it's common. Here, it's a competitive edge.

Today, Piia enjoys the lifestyle freedom she used to dream about. She earns enough to invest in the things she loves—like motorcycles and cars—but even more importantly, she has reclaimed her time. No more constant overtime. Sometimes she works a four-day week. And for the first time, she feels like she can shape her life on her own terms. As she says, "If I can build this, I can build anything."

What once felt like success—€8K months—now feels like a stepping stone. She's thinking bigger, planning strategically, and stepping fully into the CEO role her business needs.

Piia's journey is a reminder that a creative business becomes scalable the moment the founder stops trying to do everything alone. Systems, structure, and delegation freed her from the solopreneur trap—and allowed her to build a business that works, grows, and delivers results without relying on her every minute.

You Can't Delegate Chaos

My failed season of scaling also taught me one more thing: You can't delegate chaos.

For years, I had fantasized about hiring someone who would just "figure it out." A magical operations manager who would sweep in, create order out of my whirlwind ideas, and scale the business for me while I focused on the fun parts. But delegation doesn't work that way.

If there's no clarity, no process, no system, there's nothing to hand off. You can't outsource something you haven't defined. You can't expect someone to build a plane mid-flight while you keep tossing on more passengers and demanding the ride be smoother. That's not leadership—that's panic disguised as progress.

I was too quick to the draw. The truth is, I tried to scale before the business was ready. Before *I* was ready. That's one of the biggest takeaways from this entire chapter: Speed without structure creates chaos, not growth.

Eventually, I had to do the unglamorous work of slowing down. I took sales calls myself, not because I loved it (even though I do love sales), but because I needed to understand the process before I could teach someone else. I tested marketing messaging. I documented what worked. I refined before I delegated.

Simplifying might not be as exciting as hiring a big team or announcing a new launch, but it's the only way to build something that lasts. When the foundation is strong, delegation becomes a multiplier instead of a mess.

Key Takeaways

#1. Don't scale before your business is organized.

If I could go back, I'd tell myself: *Early success doesn't mean "go bigger now"—it means "get your house in order first."* When you find product-market fit, you are ready to scale, but only if your systems, roles, and processes can support that growth. The problem wasn't that we scaled—it's that we scaled before the business was truly organized to handle it.

#2. Hire the support you actually need, not the title that looks impressive.

I thought I needed an operations manager, when what I really needed was an executive assistant. Giving someone a "manager" title too early created mismatched expectations and unnecessary complexity. The right first hire is often someone who clears admin clutter—not someone tasked with running the business.

#3. **Fear of letting people down costs more than letting them go.**
I kept people on longer than I should have because I didn't want to hurt anyone's feelings. But your team represents you, and your standards must rise as your business grows. If you wouldn't rehire someone today, they may not be the right fit for tomorrow.

#4. **Know whether you're a builder or a service provider.**
If you love building a company, you're a builder. If you thrive in direct client work, you're a service provider. Scaling becomes easier the moment you stop trying to be both. Builders need doers to execute. Service providers need builders to structure growth. Once you know who you are, you can hire your opposite and stay in your zone of genius.

#5. **Raise your standards before you raise your goals.**
Sustainable scaling isn't about adding more—it's about expecting more. Every business rises to the level of its standards, not its ambitions. When you stop tolerating misalignment—whether in clients, hires, or habits—everything starts to move faster. The moment you raise your standards, you raise the ceiling on what's possible.

Strategies & Tools

Here are some practical tools you can use to avoid the solopreneur traps and set yourself up for sustainable growth. These aren't abstract ideas; they're the same strategies I leaned on (sometimes later than I should have) to bring order to the chaos of scaling.

There are three tools worth focusing on here:

The Smart CEO Delegation Model

One of the biggest questions entrepreneurs face is *what to delegate, and when.* Most people get this wrong. They delegate based on what feels urgent, not what actually frees their time. But scaling sustainably is about following the right sequence.

Here's the simple rule that guides everything: *Buy back your time before you try to grow your business.*

The mistake most entrepreneurs make is skipping ahead. They hire salespeople or marketing help while they're still the ones doing all the delivery. What happens next? The new sales team brings in more clients, the founder's already-packed schedule explodes, and instead of growth, they get burnout.

To avoid that trap, use the Smart CEO Delegation Model. It's designed around one goal: free the founder's time *first*, then scale.

- **Step 1—Admin (buy back time first):** Start by delegating administrative tasks—scheduling, invoicing, data entry, document handling, travel coordination, and bookkeeping. These are low-impact but time-intensive. They drain hours without driving growth. The right executive assistant can instantly give you back ten–twenty hours a week, time you can reinvest into strategy, clients, and sales.
- **Step 2—Client Delivery (create capacity for growth):** Once your admin is off your plate, your next bottleneck is delivery. At this stage, hire part-time or full-time support to handle elements of client work, onboarding, reporting, or customer service. This doesn't remove you from delivery completely—it just gives you breathing room. You'll have the time and capacity to sell more without breaking what's already working.
- **Step 3—Sales and Marketing (drive cash flow):** Now that your back-end and delivery are supported, you can safely delegate front-end activities like sales calls, lead management, and content creation. You're no longer forced to choose between serving clients and signing new ones. Because the business can now handle increased demand, every new sale actually adds revenue—not stress.
- **Step 4—Leadership (scale through systems, not hustle):** Only after these three foundations are solid should you delegate leadership. This includes roles like operations managers,

department leads, and project managers who oversee others. At this point, your focus shifts from running the business to steering it—setting vision, direction, and standards.

When I first started delegating, I skipped straight to Step 3 because that's where I saw the fastest cash flow. Later, I jumped to hiring an operations manager (Step 4) before having proper admin or delivery support in place. The result? More pressure, not less. Every decision flowed back to me anyway. Now I understand the sequence matters more than the speed.

You can always make more money—but you can't make more time.

Delegating in this order builds stability before scale. It gives you the freedom to focus on what truly moves the business forward—without getting buried in what keeps it merely running.

Your Zone of Genius Checklist

The second tool is about clarity. Before you can delegate effectively, you have to understand your own role. Your *zone of genius* is the work that energizes you, the work you could do all day without burning out. It's where your creativity, flow, and impact naturally come together.

Use the checklist below to define that—and just as importantly, to identify what belongs on someone else's plate:

- What could you do and never get bored with?
- Where do you find your flow state?
- What would your dream work week look like?
- How can you do it in a way that brings the most results to the business?
- What's left over? List those activities, and categorize them for delegation.

This isn't just theory—it's a design principle for how to build your company. I believe it's possible to create a business where you only do the things you love—the work that fascinates and energizes you. That should be the ultimate goal of hiring: to structure your business so that everyone, including you, gets to operate in their zone of genius.

For example, I didn't enjoy running team meetings, so I delegated them. Someone else now leads those sessions with clarity and enthusiasm, and it's a win for everyone. They get to shine in an area they enjoy, and I stay focused on the work that fuels me most.

When you use this checklist, don't just ask what you *can* delegate—ask what you *should*. Every task that drains your energy is an opportunity to build a smarter, more intentional business.

The Future Org Chart

A Future Org Chart is your hiring roadmap. Even if you're a team of one today, this sketch shows the *roles* you'll eventually need so you can stay in your zone of genius as the company grows. Below is a simplified view of what a fully built service business looks like—and the responsibilities each role owns.

Vision and Leadership

Founder/CEO (Your Zone of Genius)
- Sets direction, brand positioning, and long-term strategy
- Creates thought leadership (book, YouTube, keynotes)
- Owns key relationships and partnerships
- Reviews KPIs with leadership

COO / Operations Director
- Turns the vision into systems, priorities, and execution
- Oversees performance, delivery, and accountability
- Runs team meetings + manages the scorecard

Revenue Engine
This is the Growth Zone: marketing, sales, and client retention.

Marketing
- *Marketing Manager / Content Strategist*—leads content strategy, analyzes performance, manages creatives
- *Copywriter / Content Producer*—writes hooks, emails, scripts, and sales copy
- *Media Buyer / Ads Manager*—runs paid traffic and optimizes campaigns

Sales
- *Sales Director* (optional at scale)—leads team and KPIs
- *Closers*—run enrollment calls and close clients
- *Setters*—book qualified calls and nurture leads

Client Success
- *Head of Client Success*—owns retention, renewals, and client health
- *Client success managers*—deliver consultation and support, renewals, upsells, and referrals

Delivery and Operations
This is the Support Zone: systems, admin, finances, and tech.

Operations
- *Executive Assistant*—manages CEO calendar, admin, coordination
- *Finance*—bookkeeping, monthly reporting, cashflow
- *Tech and Automation*—CRM, automation, funnel tracking (in-house or outsourced)

You don't need all these roles right now. A Future Org Chart simply gives you a clear picture of what your business will look like when it's fully built. It helps you identify the next hire based on where bottlenecks are forming, delegate work intentionally instead of reactively, and protect your time so you can stay in the Founder's Zone of Genius.

Final Thoughts

Today, our team looks very different. By 2025, we've streamlined to nine people: an appointment setter, two sales closers, an executive assistant, two client success managers, an operations manager, a media buyer, and me. It's leaner, stronger, and built on systems that allow the business to run smoothly without me hovering over every detail. Last year, I even tested it when I stepped away for a two-week holiday to Thailand, and everything kept moving without interruption.

My business would continue if I got hit by a bus.

But a strong team alone isn't enough. To lead a business that can thrive without you, you have to evolve too. In the next chapter, we'll explore what it takes to shift from being the doer of all things to becoming the kind of leader who inspires, empowers, and drives lasting growth.

CHAPTER 5
LEADERSHIP—FROM DOER TO LEADER

There's a moment in every entrepreneur's journey when the very thing that once made you successful—doing it all yourself—becomes the thing holding you back.

In the early days, being the doer feels natural. You know your product, you know your clients, and you can deliver better than anyone else. But as the business grows, that same habit of doing turns into a bottleneck.

That was the crossroads I found myself at when it came to sales. For six months, I had personally run every sales call, refining the process until it worked like clockwork. I knew the script, I knew the objections, and I knew how to close. And I was good at it. But when it came time to let someone else step in, I hesitated.

Could anyone else really convert at the same level I could?
Could I trust someone else with something so critical?

If I wanted to build a business that didn't depend on me, however, I had to stop thinking like a doer and start growing into a leader.

In this chapter, we'll explore what it takes to make that shift—from being the doer who holds everything together, to stepping into the role of leader who builds systems, empowers people, and frees the business to grow beyond one person's capacity.

It's one of the hardest transitions in entrepreneurship, and also one of the most transformative.

Learning to Trust and Let Go

After I had delegated some of the core areas of the business—bringing in an operations manager, having an appointment setter book my calls, and onboarding a client success manager to handle the group coaching—I finally felt ready to let go of the sales calls too. Up until then, I had been the one closing all the deals, which gave me full control but also tied up a significant amount of my time.

I'd been doing that for about six months straight, taking calls every single week, always at the same time. It allowed me to refine the sales process step by step, turning it into something replicable. Even though the process was solid, I was nervous. I wasn't sure if someone else could close the same way I could.

Then came Zara.

She was one of our clients who had gone through the program with incredible success. She'd been an entrepreneur for over a decade and knew firsthand how transformative our system could be. Zara reached out wanting to help others experience what she had. It was genuine, and she was passionate about what we were doing. At the time, she was running her own coaching program and had a 100 percent success rate. With some extra time in her schedule, she joined us as a part-time closer, taking calls three to four days a week.

I still remember the first day Zara started. My husband and I were taking a short anniversary trip to Tallinn, Estonia. We were sitting in the sun at a café, and I opened my calendar. For the first time, there were no sales calls booked for me. Instead, they were all on her calendar. I felt such a deep sense of relief and freedom.

Even better, she closed two deals that very first day.

About a month later, I hired Laura, who became another long-term closer on the team. Both Zara and Laura stayed with Smart Mentoring for more than a year and were incredibly effective. It wasn't just their skills; they believed in the mission.

Even though I had hired a few other people for the sales role, the results weren't the same. Zara and Laura stood out—not because the training was different (everyone got the same training), but because they were simply the right people for the job.

They were so good, they initially made me believe that sales success was more about the person than the process.

But in time, I realized that wasn't entirely true. It's easy to think, *This one person is irreplaceable*, especially when they've been with you from the start and understand the business deeply. Zara knew the process inside and out. And yes, she was amazing, but eventually, I saw that with the right training, the same success could be replicated.

Still, hiring salespeople was never an easy decision. Every time I had to sign a new contract, I felt a wave of nerves. I'd wonder: *Is this going to work?* And with sales, it's especially risky. You're giving them leads—valuable, hard-earned leads—and if they can't close, those opportunities are wasted. Even though my sales team worked on commission (meaning they only earned when results came in), the risk wasn't just financial. It was about lost momentum, wasted leads, and missed chances to serve clients who were ready to say yes. That's what made every hiring decision in sales feel so high-stakes.

Despite the fear, if I wanted to build a company that didn't rely solely on me, I needed to let go. I couldn't spend all my time on calls, even if it meant a dip in revenue.

I had to go from doer to leader. I had to start operating like a real CEO.

My Leadership Leap

Becoming a leader didn't happen all at once. In the early days, being the doer was necessary—I had to build the sales scripts, run the calls, and deliver to clients before I could ever think about handing those things off. But once the systems were in place, the challenge shifted. It wasn't about how much I could do anymore; now it was about how well I could lead.

Some of that came naturally. I could inspire people to join the mission, and I had a knack for rallying energy. But the real work—the uncomfortable work—was learning how to hold people accountable, set boundaries, balance generosity with business sense, and let go of the idea that no one could do things as well as I could. That part I had to learn, and it didn't come easy.

To help me grow into leadership, I invested in myself. I joined a six-month leadership program with peers from different industries, which opened my eyes to the fact that every leader wrestles with similar struggles. Later, before my second baby was born, I took an even bigger leap: I invested in one-on-one leadership coaching with a $25,000 price tag. It felt like a stretch at the time, but it gave me the tools I desperately needed: operational frameworks, accountability structures, and financial discipline.

I also surrounded myself with people who modeled the kind of leader I wanted to become—friends and mentors who were direct, disciplined, and willing to tell the truth. Over time, I saw that leadership isn't something you're born with. It's something you learn with practice and trial and error.

After hiring Zara and Laura, those months were full of growth. In fact, it felt like the momentum would never end. For a short period, it was an exciting, almost magical time.

Then some challenges surfaced. Laura ended up leaving due to personal reasons. This was the time I struggled with my operations manager. And, in spring 2023, I found out I was pregnant. The combination of these blows ended up taking a toll on my mindset.

In an uncharacteristic fashion, I lowered my expectations, went into "mom mode," and focused on safety and stability rather than growth. My vision shrank from 10x goals to simply keeping things steady. With Zara still in place, I decided we only needed one closer and didn't replace Laura's role. For most of that year, I stayed out of sales calls and truly stepped into a leadership role.

Fast-forward to that summer, when things took another shift. When Zara took a six-week holiday, I jumped back in and started taking calls again. It felt like returning to the trenches after nearly a year away, but it had to be done—we still needed sales coming in, and I was now the only salesperson.

By Christmas Eve 2023, I had my baby and stepped away for the first quarter of 2024. During that time, Zara continued leading sales, but the dynamic inside the business had started to shift. Roles were changing, priorities were evolving, and by spring 2024, it was clear that what once worked smoothly no longer did. It was a tough realization, especially since she had been such a steady presence in the business.

The Myth of Solo Freedom

A common misconception I see among expert entrepreneurs is the belief that staying solo equals freedom. There's this idea that bringing on a team means more management, more responsibility, and less flexibility. I used to believe this too. But the truth is the exact opposite.

Whether you have a team or not, you'll always deal with problems. The difference is whose problems you're solving. When you operate solo, every problem lands on your plate. When you build a strong team and structure, the problems don't disappear, but your relationship to them changes. You're no longer inside every detail. You can see the business from a higher level, and the issues that come up are different from the ones you dealt with when you were working alone.

The best part is when a team member comes to you and says, "There was a problem, but I've already fixed it." That's when you know the business is no longer dependent on you for every decision.

This is why building a team is the path to freedom, not the obstacle to it. The real loss of freedom happens when you stay small, do everything yourself, and unintentionally become the bottleneck to your own growth. Solo entrepreneurship doesn't give you freedom; it just gives you a different kind of job. A job where you're the boss and the employee, the visionary and the technician, the one who dreams and the one who executes. It's an exhausting loop disguised as independence.

A lot of solopreneurs try to bypass this by automating everything with AI. And while AI is an incredible tool that can replace tasks, it can't replace ownership, intuition, or common sense. Automations can save time, but they can't think on your behalf. Real leverage comes from people who think *with* you—not tools that simply work *for* you.

True freedom comes from building support around you—humans

who can carry the weight of the mission, solve problems without you, and grow the business alongside you. Freedom doesn't come from doing less yourself; it comes from empowering others to do more with you.

Sari's Story: From "Extra Cash" Coaching to a Real Business

Sari never set out to become an entrepreneur. She worked full-time in government administration, and keto coaching was something she squeezed into her evenings for a bit of extra income. She'd run Zoom sessions after work and once created a $30 online course that a few dozen people bought. It brought in pocket money, nothing more.

"I used to say: 'Never me, I'll never be an entrepreneur.' And here I am."

Then she launched her first premium keto coaching program. On one of her early sales calls, she remembers thinking, *If I could just make $6,000 a month, that would be amazing.* But that first launch brought in more than $20,000. Seeing that number on paper shifted the idea that this was "just a side gig."

She realized she'd been playing small because she assumed she had to do everything alone and keep her offers low. With mentorship, she began letting go of the fear that she wasn't "ready" and started building structure instead of relying on sheer effort.

Within two years of officially forming her limited company in 2021, Sari had built a small but mighty team: sales consultants, an assistant, and support coaches. That transition was not smooth at first. Like so many solopreneurs, she believed she needed to be everywhere. Her fingerprints were on every decision, every client interaction, every outcome. "I thought I had to be involved in everything," she said. "But when I finally stepped back and saw that things ran just fine without me, it was freeing. Nobody ever really needed me for every task. That was only in my head."

Not only did hiring free her time—it multiplied the business. She often wonders how she ever managed on her own. The truth is, she didn't. She survived. But with a team, she grew.

Of course, she encountered several challenges. She lost $10,000 in a failed collaboration when a partner company collapsed. It stung, but it taught her to evaluate partnerships more carefully. She tested paid ads that flopped, but instead of labeling them failures, she chose to see them as experiments that simply hadn't worked *yet*. Her mindset shifted from fear of failure to curiosity about what was possible.

Leaders think that way. Doers often don't.

Once she had built systems and support, her revenue reflected it almost immediately. In her first six months of business, she made $40,000 in total. But once she started hiring, and her business took off. "Last year we made $154,000. By mid-2024 we'd already passed $226,000," she said. "None of this would have been possible without people."

That statement captures the heart of leadership: It's not about taking on more yourself—it's about creating an environment where the work grows through others.

Her visibility grew too. At first, she was terrified of making videos or being seen online. She worried about looking silly or saying the wrong thing. But consistency brought confidence, and confidence built authority. She knew things had shifted when people in Facebook groups (meaning, complete strangers) began recommending her above longtime competitors. Clients came to her saying, "Everyone told me you're the best."

Today, Sari works regular hours, protects her evenings, and finally takes vacations without her laptop. "Last summer was the first time I took a holiday and didn't bring my laptop," she shared. "The team handled everything. That felt like true freedom." She now dreams of using her time and resources to focus on impact outside the business, including charity work. She's built a business that not only supports her lifestyle but expands it.

When I asked her what she would want other women entrepreneurs to know, she didn't hesitate. Hire before you think you're ready. Raise your prices, because it's usually your mindset holding you back. Protect your energy, and build systems that support your life. And perhaps the most powerful lesson of all: Let go of being indispensable.

"Clients often get better results when you trust a team," she said.

Sari used to think $20,000 months were huge. Now $50,000 feels normal. And she knows she's just getting started. Her story is proof that leadership—not doing everything yourself—is what unlocks growth, freedom, and impact. When you stop trying to be the entire business and start building the support it needs, the whole vision expands far beyond what you could have carried alone.

Going from Doer to Leader

Scaling a business isn't just about growing revenue or hiring a team—it's about growing *you*. The biggest challenge most entrepreneurs face isn't the market, the competition, or even their offers. It's making the internal shift from being the one who does everything to becoming the leader who empowers others to do it.

When you're the doer, success depends on your effort. When you step into leadership, success depends on your vision, your systems, and your ability to bring out the best in your team. That's a very different skill set for us to work on.

The transition from doer to leader is rarely smooth, so give yourself grace. It demands letting go of control, learning to trust others, and redefining what your role actually is. These changes happen with time, and they require intentional growth and new ways of thinking.

We'll explore five key shifts every entrepreneur must make to move from doer to leader.

1. Letting go: why 80 percent is good enough
2. Build systems, not stars
3. Sales training never stops
4. Sales recruiting never stops
5. Targeting the right candidates

These shifts will help you step fully into the role of CEO. Let's get into them.

Letting Go: Why 80 Percent Is Good Enough

For most entrepreneurs, sales is often the hardest area to release. You've been on every call, refined the sales pitch, and personally handled every objection. It's not just a role—it's your reputation and revenue on the line. Naturally, it feels impossible to imagine anyone else doing it as well as you.

I know I felt this deeply.

For months, I carried every sales call myself. I knew exactly what to say on the calls, and I'd invested heavily in my own sales coaching—weekly mentoring sessions, hours of role-playing, constant refinement. Letting go of those calls felt like handing over the keys to the business.

But a mentor said something that completely reframed my thinking: "It's better to have someone performing at 80 percent of your level, doing it 100 percent of the time, than for you to keep control while juggling a dozen other responsibilities."

This perspective helped me let go. My perfectionism was actually keeping the business small. If everything depended on me, we'd always be capped by my personal bandwidth.

So, when I brought on Zara, I reminded myself that my goal wasn't to find a clone of me. It was to build consistency and free up my focus. I didn't want my role to be focusing on closing every deal forever. Instead, I wanted to focus on creating a team and a system that could do it without me. Some weeks, that meant short-term revenue dips. Long term, it meant freedom and sustainable growth.

Letting go will always feel like a leap into the unknown. But if you want your business to grow beyond you, you have to stop chasing perfection and start building trust in your people and in the systems you create for them.

Which leads me to the next shift:

Build Systems, Not Stars

In the early days, I thought sales success lived and died with one person. When Zara was closing consistently, I felt safe. She was talented, driven, and deeply invested in our mission.

But over time, I realized how fragile that was.

When she went on leave, I was forced to step back in and take every sales call again. It felt like I had rewound the clock. It was hard for me to admit that I had built my business around a star performer and not a system I can pass on to the next person. I'd invested so much time and energy into training her that rebuilding felt overwhelming.

When she finally left, I had no choice but to face what I'd been avoiding. Sales couldn't hinge on one person's shoulders. It had to be about process.

At first, my "system" was little more than a Google Drive folder with a few call recordings. It was scrappy and barely structured. It worked at the time because Zara and Laura trained alongside me. They also had initiative and could figure things out. When new hires joined and struggled, I assumed they just weren't talented enough, but that simply wasn't true. My onboarding process wasn't strong enough to set anyone up for success.

So I rebuilt from the ground up. Piece by piece, I documented everything—daily workflows, sales tracking sheets, objection handling scripts, client onboarding emails. I recorded my own calls (sometimes with my baby in my arms) and created step-by-step checklists for every stage of the process.

Now, when someone new joins the team, they don't just shadow me for a few days and hope for the best. They plug into a clear, replicable system that sets them up to succeed.

Sales Training Never Stops

When I first started building a sales team, I made training a regular, non-negotiable rhythm. In addition to getting scripts and pep talks, Zara and Laura also joined me for weekly live coaching with external consultants.

Those sessions were great. They didn't just teach technique; they built confidence and reinforced our culture of growth. Every week, my team would come away with fresh strategies and the motivation to apply them right away.

Over time, the coaches changed, but the practice stayed the same. Today, our team trains with a British sales coaching company alongside other businesses. The group dynamic creates energy and cross-pollination of ideas. It reminds everyone that sales is a craft you continually sharpen, not a skill you learn once and move on from.

What's powerful about this setup is that it also frees me from having to personally train my closers every week. Sales coaching doesn't have to come solely from you as the founder—there are experts who can mentor, challenge, and develop your team while you focus on strategy and leadership.

When training is ongoing, your salespeople feel prepared and supported. Every sales team should feel this way. They also know that growth is built into their role, which creates accountability, loyalty, and an initiative for solving problems together.

Sales Recruiting Never Stops

If there's one role you should always recruit for, it's sales. I wish I had known to do this earlier. For a long time, I treated recruitment as something I'd deal with "later."

No one stays forever, though.

When Zara went away on leave, I had to step back in and cover sales—all because I didn't have more than one salesperson. I should have been recruiting from day one, even when things felt stable.

Ideally, you should maintain at least two closers at all times—one fully ramped and performing independently, and another still in training. This creates built-in redundancy so your business doesn't grind to a halt if someone leaves, takes time off, or needs additional support. Think of it like a relay race: When one salesperson passes the baton, there's always another ready to run. Without that overlap, you risk sudden gaps that disrupt revenue and create unnecessary stress.

Recruiting for sales is about preparation. It's not just about hiring when you're short-staffed—it's about building a steady pipeline of potential closers so you're never caught off guard. This can be as simple as keeping a sales position open on your website year-round or occasionally emailing your list to let people know you're always looking for talented sales professionals. That way, when you suddenly need someone to step in, you already have a backlog of qualified contacts to reach out to.

I learned this firsthand in my previous corporate role as a sales recruiter. My job was to bring in new candidates every single week for door-to-door sales. The best sales organizations are always hiring, even when they're not technically "hiring."

Targeting the Right Candidates

Even with recruiting and a strong system, not every hire will be a fit.

Recruiting commission-only salespeople in Finland has always been a challenge—there simply aren't many candidates willing to work that way. I remember one applicant who studied our training materials and immediately critiqued them, pointing out ways they could be "improved." And sure, our onboarding can always get better. But what struck me was the difference in mindset. When Zara started, she had little more than a couple of recordings, yet she jumped in, figured it out, and made it work.

That's when I realized something important: The right people thrive in environments that require initiative. The wrong people wait for everything to be handed to them. After years of interviews, I've noticed something worth sharing: Corporate-minded hires often expect structure, certainty, and step-by-step instructions, while entrepreneurial-minded hires embrace flexibility and resourcefulness. They don't just tolerate the ambiguity of a growing business. They lean into it.

This shift in perspective changed how I recruited. Instead of looking for people who wanted a comfortable job, I started looking for entrepreneurial spirits—people who wanted the freedom to operate like business owners without having to build something from scratch. Commission sales roles were perfect for that type of personality.

The combination of a solid onboarding system and the right kind of people—those who think like entrepreneurs, not employees—created the foundation for strong leadership. With the right fit in place, I could focus on setting direction and strategy while trusting my team to carry out the work with clarity and ownership.

The Inner Work of Leadership

Up to this point, we've focused on the external actions required to step into leadership—hiring, training, building systems, and creating a strong sales foundation. These are the visible parts of leadership, the things people can see from the outside. But leadership isn't just about what you build in your business; it's also about what you build within yourself. As you grow a team, you inevitably grow yourself. The challenges you face with others often reflect the growth you need to do internally.

In the beginning, control felt like the only way forward. I micromanaged, constantly asking for updates and hovering over details. When I was stressed, my team felt it—and it showed. My operations manager even admitted that my stress was making her stressed. Looking back, it wasn't only about me; at that time, I also had the wrong people in the wrong seats. But the combination created an unhealthy environment, and I had to face the reality that culture starts at the top.

If you've ever felt the need to keep your finger on everything, you'll recognize this stage. It's part fear of letting go, part survival instinct. At that point, many of the people around me weren't deeply invested in the mission; they wanted a comfortable remote job, not the challenge of building something bold. And yet, my leadership style at the time made it easier for that mediocrity to stick around.

By fall of 2023, I knew something had to change. I didn't feel confident in my leadership. Boundaries blurred, people tested limits, and I often ended up cleaning up the mess. I was too accommodating, mistaking kindness for leadership, and it left me drained. So I made the decision to hire a one-on-one mentor. To my surprise, the work wasn't just about managing systems or setting KPIs—it was about me.

For example, there was a night when I was scrolling through Slack messages at home, completely drained and frustrated. My team wasn't performing at their best, and my tolerance for mistakes was incredibly low back then. Every small thing triggered me, and I found myself voice-noting everyone, trying to fix everything at once. In reality, the team was doing their best—it was me who had created the chaos I was trying to control.

That moment became a turning point because I realized how much the team mirrored my energy. If I was stressed and reactive, they became tense and uncertain. If I was calm and confident, they followed that lead. I started to notice the same pattern at home with my daughter—she didn't respond to my words; she responded to my energy. If I was grounded, she was calm. If I was anxious, she picked it up instantly.

That's when I understood that leadership is really energy transfer. People don't follow what you say—they follow who you are being.

Today, I no longer let stress leak onto my team. I show up calm and steady, because if I'm the rock, they can focus on doing their best work. I stopped seeing leadership as something I had to be "born with." Instead, I started seeing it as a skill—one I could build through practice, reflection, and support.

What surprised me most was how much my own growth affected the quality of people I attracted. The more I held myself to a higher standard, the more talented people wanted to join me. Leadership turned out to be less about being perfect and more about creating clarity, accountability, and trust. In no way am I saying I am perfect at it now either, but I'm far from the person who once thought doing everything herself was the only way.

Key Takeaways

#1. Letting go is essential for growth.

Holding on to every role—especially sales—keeps you stuck in the weeds. Accept that others may perform at 80 percent of your level but with 100 percent focus. Delegating critical tasks frees you to focus on vision and strategy, allowing the business to grow beyond your personal capacity and energy.

#2. Build systems that outlast people.
If success depends on one star performer, your business is fragile. Create documented processes, clear onboarding, and repeatable systems so anyone can step in and succeed. When results rely on structure rather than individuals, you gain stability, scalability, and freedom to lead instead of constantly managing emergencies or filling gaps yourself.

#3. Prioritize continuous training and recruiting.
Training and recruiting aren't one-time events. Ongoing coaching keeps your team sharp and connected to company goals. Always recruit proactively, keeping at least one person fully trained and another ramping up. This ensures stability during turnover, prevents desperate hiring, and keeps sales momentum strong no matter what challenges arise.

#4. Hire entrepreneurial-minded people who make your life easier.
The best hires don't wait for direction—they think like business owners. They take initiative, solve problems, and see what needs to be done before you have to say it. Entrepreneurial-minded people create clarity and momentum because they take responsibility instead of adding to yours. They understand that their job isn't just to do tasks—it's to make the business, and your life as the CEO, run smoother. The wrong fit might be skilled, but if they drain your time or energy, they're not the right person for the role.

#5. Leadership starts with inner work.
Your mindset sets the tone for your team. When you show up calm, clear, and consistent, it creates trust and accountability. As you grow personally—setting boundaries, releasing control, and leading with clarity—you attract stronger talent and build a culture where excellence can thrive, without you carrying every burden alone.

Strategies & Tools

One of the biggest upgrades in my leadership has been building systems for communication and feedback. Because we're a mostly remote company, I wanted to make sure the team felt connected and supported, not left on an island. So we created structured frameworks for both weekly meetings and monthly one-on-ones. Here are the three core systems we use:

Weekly Leadership Review (Feedback Loop)

A thirty-minute ritual (led by the operations manager) where the team checks in on progress, priorities, and needs. Each person shares:

- Their biggest win of the week
- Top three priorities
- KPIs (calls, hours, outcomes)
- Current capacity (maxed out, at 70–80 percent, or able to take on more)
- A happiness rating from 1–10

This keeps a real-time pulse on morale and workload, even in a remote environment.

Team Onboarding Checklist

One of the most powerful things we created after my leadership training in 2023 was a cultural onboarding document. Every new hire reads it when they join. It includes:

- A welcome message and our company values
- Key terminology (what our programs are called, what "SOP" means, etc.)
- Meeting protocols (weekly check-ins, monthly one-on-ones, expectations)
- Remote culture and communication norms (which Slack channels to use, what specific emoji reactions mean, when to use Notion, and so on)

- Practical details (working hours, holidays, sick leave, payroll or invoicing procedures)
- Links to all the tools we use

This simple but thorough document helps new hires feel like they're walking into a well-run organization rather than a startup "free-for-all." The most common feedback we get is: "Wow, everything is already so well documented." That makes them feel safe, supported, and set up for success. And because we want ownership in the process, team members—not me—are responsible for keeping SOPs updated when tools or workflows change.

Role Clarity Framework

We also built role clarity documents for every position. Each role comes with:

- The purpose of the role (why it exists in the business)
- Commitments (what the person is agreeing to deliver by taking this role)
- Responsibilities and areas of ownership
- KPIs that define success
- A sample daily workflow
- Links to step-by-step SOPs for completing core tasks

This prevents the "do a little bit of everything" trap and ensures each person knows exactly what they own. It also gives clarity about what's acceptable, what over-delivery looks like, and what won't be tolerated. For employees, this clarity is energizing; they understand the vision, what's expected, and how they can go above and beyond.

Clarity doesn't mean rigidity. Alongside clear expectations, we encourage creativity and problem-solving. Employees are told: "Here's the minimum standard. Here's what exceeding expectations looks like. And here's what we don't accept." But they're also encouraged to think outside the system, propose new solutions, and help improve the business. That combination—clarity plus creativity—keeps people engaged and invested.

Final Thoughts

When I first started this journey, handing over sales felt overwhelming. Sales calls carried the weight of the business, and I believed I had to personally handle every single one to protect the relationships and revenue we had built.

As the business expanded, continuing that way wasn't possible. My time and energy were spread too thin, and it became clear that growth would only happen if I learned to trust others. Giving up sales was a defining moment that required me to step into a new role as a leader.

The process was messy. I made hiring mistakes, navigated difficult conversations, and experienced moments when the client experience wasn't where it needed to be. Those challenges showed me that leadership is about building an environment where others can succeed and knowing how to support them with structure, guidance, and vision.

Over time, I discovered the value of surrounding myself with people whose skills surpassed my own and giving them space to lead. That shift allowed the business to grow beyond what I could personally manage, and it gave our clients a stronger, more consistent experience.

If there's one throughline, it's this: You attract A-players by being one yourself. The more I've stepped into vision, integrity, and steady leadership, the more capable, committed people have wanted to join me. That's the real transformation of moving from doer to leader. When you loosen your grip and empower others, you create space for your business to grow beyond you.

In the next chapter, we'll focus on how to grow your audience and generate high-quality leads so your business continues to expand in a sustainable way.

CHAPTER 6

MARKETING—GROWING AN AUDIENCE AND GENERATING LEADS

'll just run some ads and my calendar will be full! Easy.
I tried ads once, and they didn't work.
If I just hire an agency, they'll figure it out for me.

Do any of those sound familiar? Most entrepreneurs have at least one of these thoughts at some point in their journey. I know I did. Ads seemed like the magic shortcut: Spend the money, generate leads, get the clients—done.

When that didn't happen, however, I swung to the other extreme and decided ads were a waste of time altogether. *Ads don't work*, I told myself.

Both perspectives were wrong.

Ads aren't magic, but they aren't villains either. They're a tool. And like any tool, they only work when you've done the harder, messier work first: validating your offer, refining your message, and proving that you can sell it yourself. Without that foundation, no ad spend will save you.

In this chapter, we'll break down what it really takes to grow your audience and generate leads. We'll look at why organic marketing matters so much in the beginning, how to know when you're ready to invest in ads, and the steps to take so that, when you do, they actually work.

From Ads to Organic and Back Again

In the early days, I leaned heavily on ads. We ran campaigns for low-ticket offers—mini workshops, courses, small launches—and I even hired agencies to manage them. Honestly, ads felt too complicated, so outsourcing seemed like the easy answer.

And at first, there were results. Leads came in, sales happened, but it was never sustainable. I was playing the short-term game. If an ad campaign wasn't instantly profitable, I would shut it down and tell myself, *Well, ads just don't work.*

What I've since realized is that ads always work—they just don't always give you the results you want right away. At the time, I didn't fully understand what to expect from running them. That changed when I had the chance to learn about paid marketing from Sabri Suby (one of the world's top experts in performance marketing and direct response) during a private mastermind event. He explained a concept that reframed how I see advertising: Running ads isn't about making instant profit—it's about buying data. You put one dollar in, see what happens, learn from the numbers, and then use that data to make your next version better. Of course, the goal is still to make profit, but sustainable profit comes from optimization, not luck. Most campaigns won't hit right away, and that's normal. The businesses that win at ads are the ones willing to test, analyze, and iterate. You need both the *budget* and the *patience* to treat advertising as a long game, not a slot machine.

My mistake back then was my offers were priced too low, and we didn't test or refine enough. We'd launch one version, get frustrated, and give up too early.

Now I understand that ads don't fix a broken offer—they just magnify what's already there. The lesson wasn't that ads don't work. The lesson was that I wasn't patient enough to use them the way real marketers do: as a data game.

The real breakthrough came when I shifted to B2B and realized I could get clients by simply reaching out directly.

I went all-in on organic marketing. No ads, no outsourcing—just me and my team, showing up every day. For nearly two years, I lived and breathed organic lead generation. I posted daily, wrote my own content, and booked discovery calls. Those calls were gold because they were real-time market research where I could hear my ideal clients' exact words, refine my messaging, and improve my sales process.

And it worked. The business exploded. That year became our breakthrough year, with more than 1,000 percent growth, all without spending a single dollar on ads. This season taught me the most important lesson of my marketing journey:

- If you can sell it organically, you know your messaging and offer work.
- If you can't sell it organically, no amount of ads will fix it.

That's why we now tell clients to *prove it first*. Your first milestone should be $20,000 a month in consistent organic revenue. Once you hit that, ads become a way to *amplify* success, not cover up problems.

For a long time, I saw ads and organic marketing as black and white—one was "good," the other "bad." But over time, I realized it's not about one being better than the other. Both can work, *if you make them work*. You don't succeed because of ads or because of organic. You succeed because you commit to one path long enough to master it.

For two years, organic marketing worked beautifully for me. But as my second pregnancy progressed, reality hit: I couldn't keep being the one creating content every day. Organic alone wasn't scalable if it depended entirely on me. I needed a way to keep generating leads and revenue without being online. That's when I decided it was time to bring ads back into the picture, but this time, from a place of clarity, with a validated offer and proven messaging.

In June 2023, we started talking to a Finnish ad agency we'd worked with before and hired them to help with marketing. Progress was painfully slow, and ads didn't actually launch until October, a full four months after hiring them on. I was spending around $10,000 a month and barely getting any results. It felt like pouring money into a black hole. The agency was only tracking cost per lead, not actual client acquisition costs, ROAS (return on ad spend), or deeper performance metrics. But I didn't know that this was a problem back then, which is why I kept working with them for a year. Without those insights, there was no way to optimize or fix what wasn't working.

Needless to say, it was incredibly frustrating, and old thoughts crept back in: *Maybe ads really don't work*. But this time, I caught myself. I knew better. Ads *do* work, but only with the right strategy, the right tracking, and the right people running them.

Determined to make ads work for me, I set a clear intention: to find someone who had previously taken a business from $100,000 a month to $1 million a month.

Through my network, I found Ville, a Finnish media buyer experienced with American coaches. His approach was a big step up, with better tracking and systems, and for the first time, I felt relief seeing numbers that actually made sense.

Unfortunately, Ville later shifted focus to his own business, and I was forced to look for a new ad agency. Through some mastermind connections, I eventually connected with a twenty-two-year-old prodigy in the industry. Despite his age, he had years of experience and had even worked on ads for big names like Tony Robbins and Grant Cardone.

Like Ville, his team offered full transparency and strong reporting—master metric sheets, advanced tracking tools, and clear insight into where leads were dropping off. But what set them apart was their business model: no monthly retainer, only commission from profit. They believed so strongly in our business and saw it as a unique "black swan" opportunity that they tied their success directly to ours. The difference was night and day. After years of frustration and mediocre results, Smart Mentoring finally had a true partner.

Looking back, I see the full arc clearly: I began with ads as a shortcut, before my offer was proven. Then I swung to the other extreme and relied entirely on organic. Finally, I found the balance—organic for building relationships and trust, ads for scaling what already works. Ads were never the enemy nor a magic bullet. They simply required a solid foundation to succeed.

The work I did organically—hundreds of conversations, daily content, testing my message—made it possible for ads to work instantly when we turned them back on. What once felt complicated now feels simple, because the hard work has already been done.

Throughout my ad journey, I've learned that running ads isn't the hard part, because you can always find someone to push the buttons for you. The real challenge is staying close to the numbers, reading what the data is telling you, and constantly optimizing based on it.

Here are a few lessons that have shaped how I now approach paid traffic:

- **Stay in the data.** You need to understand what the numbers mean so you can make smart decisions, not just trust someone else's dashboard.
- **Look beyond lead cost.** A higher cost per lead can still be great if those leads convert into high-value clients. What matters is acquisition cost and ROI, not vanity metrics.
- **Use low-ticket offers as lead magnets.** We now sell inexpensive digital products to bring in qualified leads, which then feed directly into our high-ticket programs.
- **Get creative!** Visuals make or break performance. We constantly test new variations like batching fifteen different hooks and three versions of each video body. When our team edits and combines them, we end up with forty-five versions to test. The higher your budget, the more creative variation you need to keep performance strong.

The bottom line is that ads work, but only if you know how to work them.

Your Marketing Foundation

Marketing is the heartbeat of your business, but it's also one of the most misunderstood parts of growth. There are endless tactics you *could* try—ads, social media, funnels, events—and it's easy to get lost chasing the newest shiny thing.

Through working with hundreds of clients, I've seen that real, sustainable marketing comes down to a few timeless principles: doing the work yourself first to gain clarity, showing up consistently even when you're busy, and building habits that keep leads flowing month after month.

Let's explore how to build marketing systems that actually work.

First, Do the Work

When it comes to marketing, the temptation is always to look for the shortcut—the ad campaign, the viral reel, the quick hire who will "just handle it" for you. But there's no shortcut for clarity. Before you can outsource, automate, or scale, you have to *do the work* yourself. That means rolling up your sleeves and getting crystal clear on three things:

1. **Your offer:** what you're selling and why it matters
2. **Your audience:** who it's for and what problem you're solving for them
3. **Your message:** how you communicate your value so it resonates

Skipping this step is like building on a shaky foundation. Things may look fine in the beginning, but as soon as you add weight—more clients, a team, or paid ads—the cracks start to show, and everything becomes unstable.

When I say "do the work," I'm not talking about perfect branding or a fancy logo. I mean having real conversations with real people. Getting on calls. Listening closely to their struggles, their desires, and the exact words they use to describe their pain points. This is the unglamorous part of entrepreneurship that no agency can truly replace. Sure, there are agencies that *can* do this, but the great ones are expensive, and even then, they'll never know your audience as intimately as you. As a founder, this kind of insight is priceless. Understanding your clients at this level shapes your messaging, your offers, and your confidence when you sell.

Too often, I see business owners try to skip ahead of this work. They hire a marketing team or a virtual assistant to post for them, thinking that delegation will solve the problem. But if you don't know your own message, no one else will either. It's like trying to hire a translator when you don't even know what language you're speaking.

This is why I encourage every client to *start with organic marketing*. Not because it's free, but because it's feedback-rich. Every post you write, every DM you send, every discovery call you have is a chance to test and refine. It's immediate market research.

Here's what that looked like for me:

- I posted daily, experimenting with content and paying attention to what got traction.
- I booked dozens—eventually hundreds—of discovery calls and tracked the objections I heard most often.
- I rewrote our messaging over and over until it felt like I was speaking my ideal client's exact language.

None of that was easy. It was tedious, even exhausting at times. But it built a foundation no ad spend could replace. By the time we turned ads back on two years later, they got us leads on day one because the message had been proven.

When you do this work yourself first, you gain two powerful advantages:

- **Clarity:** You'll know exactly what works and why, which makes it easier to train others later.
- **Confidence:** You'll trust that when you invest in ads or a team, you're amplifying something solid rather than gambling on guesswork.

It's natural to want to move fast, but if you skip this stage, you'll end up paying for it later—in wasted dollars, missed opportunities, and a whole lot of frustration. So before you spend money on ads, before you hire a social media manager, before you even think about scaling, pause and ask yourself: "Have I done the work?"

Once You Start, Don't Stop

One of the best lessons I learned from one of my sales coaches was this: *Once you start generating leads organically, don't stop.*

It sounds obvious, but so many entrepreneurs fall into the trap of inconsistency. Here's how it usually plays out: You finally push yourself to start posting consistently—on Facebook, LinkedIn, or Instagram. Maybe one of your posts takes off. Comments start flooding in, your inbox fills with DMs, and suddenly you have more leads than you know what to do with.

And then you take your foot off the gas.

It feels safe to slow down because you assume the momentum will last. But before long, those initial leads dry up, and you're back at square one, scrambling for clients again. The same thing happens once people land their first five clients. They get busy delivering, stop marketing, and when those contracts end, they're left in panic mode with an empty pipeline.

It creates a stressful cycle: Scramble, sell, serve, scramble again.

I've watched this happen over and over with clients in our own twelve-week program. The first stage of marketing is exciting because results come fast, but the real work begins *after* those first few wins. That's when consistency matters most.

How to Generate Leads

There are countless ways to generate leads, and it's easy to get lost trying to figure out which tactics actually work. Over the years, I've tested many different approaches with my clients, and while there's no single perfect method, three strategies consistently rise to the top. These three have proven to be the most reliable and effective for building momentum, especially when you're looking to create a steady flow of clients without overcomplicating your marketing.

Let's get into them.

The Premium Pilot Approach

When you're starting out, you don't need to overcomplicate things. In fact, we teach our clients to focus on just one goal: Land the first five to ten clients.

Think of this strategy as a "premium pilot"—essentially a beta test for your new program or service. It's framed as a trial run, which builds trust and makes it easier for people to say yes to something unproven. For example, let's say your long-term vision is to sell a $10,000 program.

You can start by offering it at $5,000 for a small, hand-picked group of founding members. Your messaging might sound like this:

> "I'm testing a new program designed to help [your ideal client] achieve [specific result]. I'm looking for a small group of people to join me in this first round before I raise my price."

This approach works beautifully in social media posts and direct messages because it feels personal and exclusive. But—and this is important—you can't keep running the "pilot" forever. It's a bridge, not a long-term strategy. Once you've proven the offer and delivered great results for those first clients, it's time to evolve your marketing and raise your price to its full value.

Start with the Low-Hanging Fruit

Your very first clients will almost always come from people who already know you—even if just a little. Past clients, social media followers, old coworkers, friends of friends. These connections are your *low-hanging fruit*.

When I was starting out, I tapped into my own low-hanging fruit network. I messaged people on WhatsApp, reconnected with Facebook friends, and reached out to anyone who had shown even a hint of interest in my work. These conversations didn't feel "salesy." They felt natural because there was already some level of trust. Trust is the hardest thing to build with cold leads. By starting with your existing network, you shortcut that barrier and can book clients faster.

What most entrepreneurs overlook is that this is something you should return to often. Even if you already have clients or a steady pipeline, revisiting your warm network can reignite momentum when things slow down. People change jobs, gain new needs, or finally reach the point where they're ready to invest. Your low-hanging fruit grows back, so it's worth checking the tree regularly.

And don't worry if your very first paying client is someone you know personally. That doesn't make your business any less legitimate. What matters is proving that someone trusted you with their money and got results. That early social proof is gold.

Borrowing Audiences

One of the fastest ways to grow when you're just starting out is to *borrow someone else's audience*. That's exactly what I did in the early days. Instead of trying to build a following from scratch, I looked for communities that already had my ideal clients and pitched myself as a guest expert. I ran webinars for groups like Female Founders and Business and Dreams, and every time, I walked away with a flood of new leads.

Speaking engagements work the same way. Each time I've spoken at an event—whether on stage or virtually—I've gained not only leads but also credibility. This is why speaking opportunities are so powerful: They position you as an authority while also putting you directly in front of warm, ready-to-buy prospects.

If you don't yet have an audience of your own, focus on finding people who do. You can:

- Pitch to run a webinar for their community, highlighting the value you'll deliver and how it helps their members.
- Create joint ventures or collaborations where you cross-promote each other's audiences in a way that benefits both sides.
- Offer a small affiliate bonus to partners who refer leads or clients to you, giving them a reason to send people your way.

One strategy we've seen work well is using Facebook groups—even ones where direct promotion isn't allowed. By consistently adding value and connecting with people in a genuine way, you can direct them to your Instagram or other platforms where you can continue the conversation.

Borrowing audiences is a great way to skip years of slow, one-by-one outreach. By stepping into spaces where trust is already built, you can accelerate your visibility and start generating clients much faster.

Consistency Creates Stability

Once you've worked with your first five to ten clients, you've proven that your offer works. You now have testimonials, case studies, and a clear understanding of who you serve and the results you help them achieve. This is a pivotal moment.

At this stage, the focus shifts from proof to predictability. Your goal is no longer just to land a handful of clients—it's to keep a steady flow of leads coming in so you're never stuck scrambling when contracts end or a launch slows down.

The mistake many entrepreneurs make is pulling back too soon. They get busy delivering for current clients, stop marketing, and assume the momentum will take care of itself. But momentum is fragile. When you stop showing up, the pipeline dries up, and suddenly you're back at square one, hustling to fill spots.

To prevent this cycle, you need to build *repeatable systems* that run even when you're busy. These systems don't need to be complex, but they must be consistent. At minimum, they should include:

- Regular content that nurtures and attracts new leads
- A reliable way to reach out and build relationships with followers or group members
- A simple process for turning strangers into warm leads, and warm leads into paying clients

Think of this like moving from a survival mindset to a scaling mindset. You're no longer chasing one-off wins—you're building a marketing engine that works day after day.

When you keep showing up consistently, even during your busiest seasons, you create stability. That stability frees you from the constant stress of wondering where your next client will come from. It's what takes you from scattered and reactive to focused and scalable.

To make this practical, build one or two simple lead-generation systems you can maintain no matter how full your schedule gets. For example:

- Hosting a regular weekly or monthly webinar or Instagram Live to showcase your expertise
- Sending consistent email newsletters (daily or weekly) to stay connected with your audience
- Reaching out to new contacts daily on LinkedIn, Instagram, or Facebook to build authentic relationships

These are the quiet, behind-the-scenes rhythms that compound over time. In marketing—and in business—what you do consistently matters far more than what you do occasionally.

On Finding Quality Ad Agencies

Ad agencies are like mechanics. Some are fantastic and will get you where you need to go. Others are mediocre or downright terrible, and you won't know which one you've got until you ask the right questions and look at the right data.

Today, I only trust word-of-mouth recommendations when it comes to finding an agency. If someone I know and respect hasn't personally vouched for them, I move on. Here are three things I look for:

- Come highly recommended through trusted networks
- Can show you clear metrics they use to track success
- Have real, measurable wins with past clients they can point to

It's also worth mentioning that even the best agencies aren't forever. Their quality, people, and focus can change over time. I now approach agency work like a project and not a permanent partnership. At some point, you'll likely want to bring your marketing capabilities in-house, where you can control the data, the creative, and the pace of experimentation.

When we started working with the agency we use at the time of this printing, they shared a detailed master metrics sheet that tracked everything from lead cost to acquisition cost. That one document gave me confidence they were running a business built on data and results.

Unfortunately, not every experience was like that. The first company I hired charged between $2,000 and $4,000 per month, but *they didn't even know our acquisition costs*. Without that, there was no way to know if what we were doing was profitable.

Later, Ville, the second company we worked with, charged around $3,000 per month. Initially, there was no revenue share, but during a later renegotiation, I agreed to include one. That turned out to be a huge mistake. Because his percentage was based on *all* revenue, not just revenue from ads, he got paid no matter what. Whether the ads worked or not, his income was guaranteed. It was a bad structure that created misaligned incentives.

Trust me. I won't have that type of contract ever again.

But you can't expect to land a good deal if you haven't built a proven business first. When we tried to negotiate a performance-based deal with our first agency, they said no. The difference now is that we've helped more than five hundred clients and have systems that can handle growth. Agencies know if they bring us hundreds of clients, we can deliver without collapsing. Many companies can't say the same, and I've heard countless stories of businesses falling apart when they scale too fast.

That's why it's so important to *sell your vision* to your agency, not just your current numbers. When I shared my bigger vision for the company with my current ad agency, they believed in it so much they were the ones who switched to a fully performance-based model themselves.

The best people want to work with companies aiming for something significant.

Of course, not every agency operates at that level. Some pitched low-end services—like running basic LinkedIn ads for $500 per month—and when I asked about ROI or client acquisition costs, they couldn't answer. They weren't tracking anything meaningful. These agencies often sell to entrepreneurs who don't know what questions to ask, which is how they get away with mediocrity.

Knowing your numbers protects you.

At this stage, we know exactly what we're looking for: Our client acquisition cost needs to stay under $3,000 for our $8,000 offer. More importantly, we're aiming for at least a 3–10x return on ad spend. In other words, when we spend one dollar, we want at least five back, a 5x ROAS. As long as that number stays healthy, it doesn't matter how high the budget goes. At that point, as the "bro marketers" like to say, we're basically printing money.

If an agency can't operate with those numbers in mind, they're not a fit. Because they probably don't know enough of what they should be doing.

Even if someone else is running your ads, you must understand the metrics yourself. Otherwise, you'll never know if what they're doing is truly working. That's one of the biggest lessons I've learned: Hiring someone to handle ads isn't a shortcut if you don't know how to measure success.

Today, our setup looks different. Instead of relying on outside agencies, we're in the process of building our first-ever in-house marketing team. Just like we've done with sales and client delivery, we're documenting every part of our marketing system (campaigns, creative processes, metrics, workflows) so the entire engine becomes internal, repeatable, and scalable. It's the first time we've had this level of clarity in our marketing, and creating these systems now means the business will never depend on external partners in the same way again.

Social Media: Building Relationships, Not Just Followers

We can't talk about marketing without talking about social media. It's where most of your audience spends their time and often where potential clients first discover you. It's where visibility, connection, and conversation begin.

The problem is that many entrepreneurs treat it like a direct sales channel, putting too much pressure on every post to generate instant revenue. Social media works best when you view it for what it really is: a place to build *trust and relationships* that lead to sales over time.

Below are seven key principles for using social media to grow your business in a way that feels authentic and sustainable.

Choose the Right Platforms

When it comes to platforms, keep it simple. For most coaches and consultants, the core platforms are Instagram, Facebook, YouTube, and LinkedIn. TikTok can work for some audiences, but it's not essential. Remember, many people are on multiple platforms—you don't need to be everywhere. Focus your energy where your ideal clients already spend time.

The platform itself doesn't matter as much as your content, though.

Create Content That Resonates

Entrepreneurs often stress about "hacking the algorithm," but algorithms are simply reflections of human behavior. If your content sparks genuine engagement—comments, shares, and conversations—it will naturally be seen by more people. Instead of obsessing over hashtags or tricks, focus on creating content that resonates.

And when it comes to content, here's the golden rule: *Don't sell on social media.*

That might sound counterintuitive, but your goal isn't to push your offers or list program details. The goal is *visibility*—getting eyeballs on you and your business. Rather than asking, "How can I sell here?" ask, "What can I post that people will find interesting enough to comment on or share?"

The posts that perform the best are often the ones that feel the most vulnerable or scary to publish. Vulnerability creates connection, and connection leads to trust.

When your content is truly impactful, it goes beyond likes. It makes people take action. Sometimes, it even inspires them to change something in their business or life—*before* they've ever paid you.

I've had people tag me saying they were inspired by my free content to launch their own "$10,000 in ten days" challenge. They weren't even clients yet; they simply watched a YouTube video and took action.

That's the power of impactful content: When someone gets a result just from engaging with what you share, they're naturally going to want to go deeper and work with you.

Treat Content Like a Science Experiment

Too many entrepreneurs hesitate to post because they worry about how it will be received. A better approach is to think like a scientist:

- Post consistently.
- Watch what happens.
- Measure, learn, and adjust.

This scientific approach removes the pressure of perfection. Over time, you'll see clear patterns around what works and why. If a post sparks comments, conversations, or leads to a client, that's data worth repeating. If a post falls flat, that's also valuable data. Pivot, tweak, and try a new angle.

This mindset removes the pressure to be perfect and helps you identify patterns over time. You'll start to see clearly which topics, formats, or stories resonate most with your audience—and why.

Measure What Actually Matters

When tracking your social media results, don't stop at surface-level metrics like impressions or views. Impressions only tell you how many people saw the post, not whether it moved them closer to becoming a client. Leads, on the other hand, show real progress: who commented, messaged you, or showed genuine interest.

Pay special attention to:

- Which posts your paying clients saw before deciding to buy
- Which content generated direct messages or inquiries from potential clients

Impressions still matter—they can help you identify attention-grabbing hooks. For example, if one post generates leads and another gets high impressions, combine the best parts of both: the hook from one and the call-to-action from the other.

This focus keeps you centered on what matters most: high-quality leads, not vanity metrics.

Build a Foundation for Scaling with Ads

Social media begins as an organic growth tool, but over time, it becomes the testing ground for scaling with ads.

At that mastermind with Sabri Suby, he explained that most entrepreneurs are playing too small. They're busy tracking followers, counting likes, and celebrating small engagement spikes, thinking those numbers mean growth. But none of that moves the needle if you want to scale to millions.

The real players think differently. Instead of measuring likes, the businesses that grow the fastest know their data. They track:

- Client acquisition cost
- Return on ad spend (ROAS)
- Sales cycle length

When you understand these numbers, there's no more guessing. Scaling becomes a numbers game where you spend one dollar and know how much comes back.

Aim to Be a Key Person of Influence

One of the most powerful mindset shifts I've had came from something Daniel Priestly shared on *Diary of a CEO*: As an entrepreneur, you don't need to be a mainstream influencer; you need to be a *key person of influence*. That means you don't need hundreds of thousands of followers to build a thriving business. Even five thousand people who truly know, like, and trust you can be enough to create consistent revenue and long-term success.

I used to obsess over vanity metrics—follower counts, likes, views. But over time, I realized those numbers don't necessarily translate into impact or income. A post with only five likes can still be incredibly powerful if it speaks directly to your ideal client and strengthens your brand.

Here's something you may not know: Premium clients usually aren't the ones commenting or liking. They're lurkers—quietly watching, evaluating, and deciding whether to trust you. When they're ready, they'll reach out. That's why consistency and quality matter so much more than chasing big numbers. Social media isn't about being famous. It's about being trusted. And if you can build influence with the right audience, even a small following can fuel a very big business.

Beware of Comparison and Trolls

One of the easiest traps to fall into with social media is comparison. You scroll through Instagram or LinkedIn and think, *Her content is better than mine. I should be posting like him. Their strategy must be the secret to success.*

But you don't really know what's happening behind the scenes. Many of the entrepreneurs you see online aren't even running their own accounts. Someone else is posting for them, curating their feed, and managing their brand presence. They're not in the comments; they're not worrying about trolls—they understand the game and stay focused on the bigger picture.

The more time you spend comparing yourself to others, the less time you spend creating content that serves your audience. Someone else's system might be perfect for *them*, but that doesn't mean it's right for you.

In the early days, posting in Facebook groups worked incredibly well for me. But along with the leads and visibility came something I wasn't prepared for: negativity. In December 2022, I was in Los Angeles for a business event, which was supposed to be one of the highlights of the year. Instead, I was lying in a hotel bed with a fever, watching my social media erupt into a storm. Overnight, negative discussions, harsh opinions, and criticism flooded in about my business.

I was horrified. I couldn't believe people would say such nasty things. It felt so personal. It felt awful. Not because clients were leaving (sales were actually increasing), but because success brings visibility, and visibility brings noise. If you're running ads or reaching a wider audience, trolls will always show up. They're a sign you're reaching more people.

In another incident, a journalist reached out looking for controversy. They even contacted some of our clients to "investigate" and eventually published a clickbait article, despite finding no real story to tell.

I went through stages with these situations. At first I was shocked. I was scared of what it might mean. But then nothing important changed afterward. Our clients were still getting results, my team kept working, and my family was safe. The shock existed only in my head.

Next, I ignored them. I decided not to read the discussions. I posted and logged out, focusing on my own work and letting others post what they wanted to post. Finally, when my energy returned, I began to accept but reframe the situation. I replied to some comments and noticed something: the more people talked, the more our message spread, which led to more sales, more media coverage, and more followers.

And guess what? Troll comments actually help the algorithm. They create more engagement, which boosts visibility. In a strange way, trolls can work in your favor, as long as you don't let them drain your energy.

Another valuable lesson has been shifting how I think about my social media feed. I once assumed it was about sharing what *I* wanted to post. But the most successful brands think differently.

For example, I follow a coach with nearly a million Instagram followers. Her feed looks like a beautifully curated Pinterest board, designed entirely around the aspirations of her ideal client. Every post is crafted to reflect what her audience wants to see and feel, not just what she feels like sharing.

This is what turning social media into business media looks like.

Authenticity still matters, of course. But strategy matters too. Platforms like Instagram, LinkedIn, and Facebook are perfect for aspirational, lifestyle-driven content, while long-form platforms like YouTube or podcasts are better suited for teaching and deep dives.

Think about brands like Red Bull or Apple. Their feeds aren't filled with product shots or sales pitches. Instead, they showcase a lifestyle—an identity their audience wants to be part of. That's the mindset to adopt: Focus less on comparison or critics, and more on creating a brand presence that inspires, connects, and grows your audience.

Long-Term Thinking

One of the biggest shifts I've made is embracing long-term thinking. It's a theme that runs through every part of business growth, but it's especially important when it comes to marketing.

When you commit to creating a post every day—or batching thirty posts in one day—you're not just chasing quick wins. You're building skills: learning copywriting, practicing how to engage, becoming more comfortable on camera, and refining how you present your ideas. Each post is an investment in your future self—the leader who commands authority, gets invited to big stages, and inspires trust with both clients and your team.

For me, it's no longer about whether one post goes viral. It's about the discipline of showing up, knowing that every piece of content makes me stronger than I was last month. I've been sharing content for more than a decade now, and I still haven't "cracked the code," because there is no code to crack. Success comes from consistent improvement and a willingness to play the long game.

That's why it's unrealistic to expect clients to magically show up at your door. Even Apple, one of the most recognizable brands in the world, still invests heavily in marketing. If they can't coast, neither can we.

One of my YouTube strategists once told me that it takes six to nine months of posting two high-quality videos per week just to reach your first 1,000 subscribers. That gave me perspective. Too often, we're sold the illusion of overnight success—"10,000 followers in 30 days!"—and that creates impatience. Growth takes time! After ten months of uploading weekly, as of the time of this writing, I have 565 subscribers—and only now do I feel like I'm beginning to understand what works on this platform. It's a long game. Give yourself time: a year or more before you judge the outcome.

When you focus on the long term, your approach changes. Growth, excellence, and service become your true metrics—not just likes, comments, or this month's revenue. And here's the beautiful part: The people you attract will reflect that same mindset. Clients, team members, and even partners like ad agencies will be drawn to the vision you're building.

Short-term thinking brings short-term results. Long-term thinking builds something lasting. It changes not only your strategy, but also the kind of people who want to join you on the journey.

Key Takeaways

#1. Validate your offer organically before spending on ads.
Ads don't fix a broken offer, they amplify what's already working. If you can't sell it organically through direct conversations and content, no amount of ad spend will magically make it profitable. Nail your messaging, sales process, and delivery first, then use ads to scale.

#2. Build a predictable pipeline.
A stable business isn't built on one-off bursts of marketing. Create simple, repeatable systems that keep leads flowing consistently, even when you're busy serving clients. This steady pipeline protects you from the feast-or-famine cycle and gives you the confidence to grow sustainably.

#3. Social media is for connection, not selling.
The goal of social content isn't to pitch your offer; it's to build trust and spark engagement. The posts that feel the most vulnerable or personal often perform best. Think of your social channels as visibility platforms, not sales pages.

#4. Borrow audiences to grow faster.
When you don't yet have a large audience, leverage someone else's. Webinars, collaborations, podcasts, and speaking engagements allow you to reach warm leads more quickly while also positioning yourself as an authority in your space.

#5. Play the long game.
Overnight success is a myth. Marketing mastery comes from consistent effort over months and years—testing, learning, and improving. When you focus on long-term growth rather than quick wins, you'll naturally attract the right clients, team members, and partners to support your vision.

Strategies & Tools

A key strategy for lead generation is having a *systematic content process*. I spent a long time testing different approaches until I found one that worked efficiently without me creating posts every single day. Here's what worked best:

Batch-create 30 content pieces in one day.

- 10 short-form "talking head" videos (TikTok/Reels style) where I spoke freely on a topic. These built trust and showed my expertise.
- 10 viral-style clips with strong hooks and B-roll (for example: "I don't know who needs to hear this, but it's easier to sell a $10,000 offer than a $1,000 offer"). These grabbed attention and brought new eyeballs.
- 10 reposts of the best-performing content from the previous month.

With this system, I could create a month of content in just four to six hours. Later, I brought in a marketing assistant to help with editing and captions, but at first it was just me batching everything. The most important part was making sure every piece of content included a clear call to action—whether it was to comment, DM me, or grab a free resource. That consistency kept new leads coming in.

I also learned that you pay either with your time (organic) or with your money (ads). With organic, you need to stay consistent and proactive. For example, I had a team member messaging everyone who commented or followed me to start conversations. We also used LinkedIn automations to connect with new people regularly. That outreach piece is crucial: Don't just sit and wait for people to come to you. Proactively start conversations with new followers, commenters, or connections. The more conversations you have, the more opportunities you'll create for booked calls—and ultimately, more clients.

Final Thoughts

Looking back, my marketing journey was never about ads versus organic—it was about learning to understand my audience and understanding what triggers them to take action. In the beginning, I chased quick wins, thinking I could skip the messy middle by outsourcing or pouring money into ads. What I didn't realize then was that every conversation, every post, and every early client was laying the foundation for something bigger.

Marketing is about building trust, shifting beliefs, and guiding people to take the next step in your sales process. It's about showing up consistently, testing ideas, and staying committed even when the results aren't immediate. When you play the long game and keep your pipeline flowing, you don't just grow your audience—you grow your confidence as a business owner.

Now that you've seen how to generate leads and build demand, it's time to turn that attention into sales. In the next chapter, we'll dive into selling with confidence and creating a system that allows you to grow without burning out—so you can turn those leads into loyal, paying clients.

CHAPTER 7

SALES—SELLING WITH CONFIDENCE AND SYSTEMIZING GROWTH

Most people run from sales.
I ran toward it.

When other teenagers were scooping ice cream or stocking shelves, I was selling candy at the market, offering product tastings in grocery stores, and even cold-calling strangers as a telemarketer. It wasn't glamorous, but it taught me one of the most valuable lessons in business: Companies need people who can sell.

I noticed early on that when I leaned into that skill, when I wasn't afraid to say, "I like sales, and I'm good at it," doors opened. At eighteen years of age, a manager even told me the reason I got hired was because I liked sales. While others tried to hide from sales or frame themselves as "customer service," I embraced it.

That mindset became my edge. It shaped how I approached every opportunity that followed—and it's why, even now, I believe mastering sales is the foundation for building and scaling any business.

In this chapter you'll learn how to approach sales as the lifeblood of your business—not something to dread or outsource too soon. We'll explore why sales is really about service, how to sell your offer with confidence, and why you, as the founder, must be the first and best salesperson for your business.

Sales Is About Serving

Most entrepreneurs start their businesses because they want to help people, not because they love selling. But sales *is* helping people. When done well, sales is about guiding someone toward the solution they need and empowering them to take action.

Early in my journey, I didn't fully understand this.

I knew I was naturally influential. If I was genuinely excited about something, I could sell the idea. But when it came to selling my own services, especially at a premium price, I froze. I'll never forget my first webinars. I had my slides, my script, and my structure down perfectly. I rushed through every word, my voice shaky and fast, just wanting to get it over with.

And this didn't happen just once. For at least a dozen webinars, I struggled through the same cycle—teaching confidently for forty-five minutes, then feeling awkward and nervous during the pitch. I told myself people came to learn, not to be sold to, so the moment I shifted into sales, it felt uncomfortable.

The turning point came when I realized the people attending my webinars—sometimes hundreds at a time—weren't just there for free information. They were there because they were struggling. They needed *real change*. An hour of teaching wasn't going to transform their lives. The only way to serve them fully was to offer a next step.

That was the moment sales stopped feeling like pressure and started feeling like service.

Seeing sales as serving helped me approach every conversation as a win-win. It shifted my focus from trying to "close" someone to genuinely helping them make a decision that serves their goals.

In the sections ahead, we'll look at how to put this mindset into practice—how to focus on the right people, navigate the personal emotions tied to pricing, and bring confidence and clarity to your sales process. These principles will help you build a sales approach that feels natural, ethical, and effective.

Only Sell to People Who Want the Help

A surprising truth about sales: People *want* you to make an offer.

I learned this during a webinar I hosted for my university alumni group. I gave a full hour of valuable content but didn't mention anything about working with me. At the end, every question was about my business and my services. They were practically begging for the details I hadn't given them.

That experience flipped my thinking. If someone is showing up for a training on a specific topic, they're already interested. They've raised their hand to say, "I need help." Failing to offer a solution is actually frustrating to them.

These days, we don't sell directly during these webinars. Instead, we use them to invite attendees to book a call. That way, the actual sales conversation happens privately, and only with people who are a strong fit.

Selling Your Services Feels Personal

Even though I'd been selling for years—B2B, telemarketing, promotions—nothing prepared me for selling my *own* services.

Selling for a company is easy in comparison. If someone says no, they're rejecting the company, not you. But when it's *your* offer, *your* business, it feels deeply personal. It's like they're saying *you* aren't worth it.

I see this all the time with our clients. Many have long, successful careers as top salespeople inside major organizations. They can sell millions in products or services for their employer. But the moment they have to sell their own coaching, consulting, or creative work, their confidence crumbles. Why is that?

Because now, the price feels like a reflection of their self-worth.

That's why entrepreneurship is such a deep self-development journey. You can't separate your inner growth from your outer success. If you don't truly value yourself, it will show up in your sales conversations.

The shift comes when you realize that people aren't paying *you*. They're paying for a transformation. They're paying to solve a problem that's holding them back. When you see it in this manner, you stop apologizing for your prices and start confidently guiding clients toward change.

The Energy You Bring to Money

Money is neutral. The meaning you attach to it comes from you.

If you think of money as dirty or sales as sleazy, every conversation will carry that energy. But if you see money as a tool—a way to care for yourself, your family, your community, and your future—it becomes something positive.

I've had people on social media comment that no one would ever pay the prices we charge, accusing us of being "too expensive." But pricing should have nothing to do with what strangers think and everything to do with *your* belief.

Which leads me to pricing.

Price with Confidence

I was on a group call with a consultant debating whether I should raise my rates, so I raised my hand and asked, "Should I go for the higher number or stay where I am?"

"Go with the number you actually believe in, because your results will be better," he responded.

He was right. If you name a price you don't fully believe in, it shows. Your voice tightens, your energy dips, and the client can feel it instantly. Now, whenever my own clients ask me about raising their prices, I share the same principle. Even if we recommend they charge more, if they don't believe in that higher number yet, we start with what feels comfortable. Once they get quick wins at that level, their confidence grows and raising prices later becomes natural, not forced.

When I started, my first online course was $150. Even then, some people told me it was "too much." Now we sell offers at ten times that price, and clients happily pay because they see the value.

Pricing isn't just for you either; it's also symbolic for your clients. The more people pay, the more they pay attention. When someone invests at a higher level, they show up differently. They're more committed, more engaged, and more likely to follow through. Charging premium prices isn't just about earning more; it's about creating transformation on both sides.

When our clients start working with us, they often feel unsure about charging premium rates. They've been told by friends, family, or even other business owners that "no one will ever pay that much." But we help them test it. And almost every time, they're shocked to discover that people *do* pay. This shift builds confidence as much as it increases revenue. Once you see someone happily pay for your service, you stop over-explaining or apologizing for your prices.

Sell It Yourself Before You Scale

In the beginning, you *are* the business. No one knows your clients like you do—their pain points, dreams, and hesitations live inside your head because in many cases you've lived them yourself. That insight can't be outsourced.

Not yet, at least.

When you're first starting out, you might feel unprepared for sales. Many brilliant entrepreneurs do. They're exceptional at their craft but have never had to sell themselves before. It feels foreign, even intimidating. But sales isn't a personality trait—it's a skill set. And like any skill, it can be learned.

The only way to build that skill—and the confidence that comes with it—is by doing the work. Confidence doesn't just appear because you repeated affirmations or told yourself to "feel ready." It's built through proof: one call at a time, one client at a time. Even the calls that end in a "no" matter. They're reps. Each conversation helps you refine your offer, sharpen your messaging, and understand your clients on a deeper level.

I think about a young photographer we worked with. She was incredibly talented but had almost no entrepreneurial experience. At first, selling her services felt impossible. She second-guessed everything and even considered quitting. Instead of giving up, we gave her a different kind of opportunity: photographing two of our live events. Seeing people respond to her work, getting immediate feedback, and proving to herself that she could deliver transformed her mindset. Once she had that proof, she began closing deals with a level of authority she didn't have before.

That's how confidence grows—not by sitting at home thinking about your skills, but by using them.

Early on, your first ten to fifteen sales calls should be treated as practice, not pressure. Think of them as data-gathering sessions. Go in to listen and learn. Use what you hear to tweak your process and improve your pitch. These early conversations are where you discover what truly resonates and what falls flat. They're also where you begin to see your own value reflected back to you through the eyes of your clients.

Here's where many founders make a mistake: They try to delegate sales too soon. They hire a salesperson, hoping that person will handle everything. But if you can't sell your offer yourself, it's nearly impossible for someone else to sell it for you.

In the beginning, sales is something you have to own. You need to know your numbers, understand your clients' objections, and feel the rhythm of what makes your offer convert. But this isn't forever—it's a stepping stone. Once you've proven the process and built predictable results, you can start building a system that runs without you.

That's now how my business operates today. I don't train new closers, recruit salespeople, or lead team meetings anymore. We have a sales team lead who does all of that. My role is simply to look at performance reports and make strategic decisions. That's the vision I want you to have: a business that sells, grows, and thrives without needing you in every deal.

Whether you love sales or not, you must embrace it in the early days. Because once you master selling your own product, you'll have the clarity and confidence to teach others how to scale it with you.

Anni's Story: From Hustling PT to Five-Figure Weeks with a Team

When I think about what's possible when you embrace sales, raise your prices, and let yourself grow into a leader, I often think of Anni. She started her career as a personal trainer in Berlin, not in a studio of her own, but bouncing from parks to gyms to people's living rooms. Some mornings she'd wake up at five to teach a bootcamp across the city, then spend the rest of the day riding trains and buses to her next sessions. It was exhausting work, physically and mentally, but she loved what she did.

Still, she knew that this lifestyle had an expiry date. "I kept thinking: I'm great at what I do. But if I stop working, everything stops. I wanted to build something bigger than myself."

Before the pandemic, she'd made a $70 online course, but it felt more like a hobby than a business. The real turning point came when she finally invested in mentorship. Her mentor suggested pricing her new program at $997, and she remembers laughing out loud at the idea. "I was convinced nobody in Finland would ever pay that much for an online fitness program."

She started smaller—$400 for a beta round—and even that number stretched her. But her clients got real results, results they couldn't get anywhere else. They wanted more. And so she raised the price, then raised it again. Eventually, she sold the exact same program for nearly triple—and people continued to buy, because the value was there.

Her confidence grew as her sales grew. Through consistent content, simple conversions, and a mindset shift around worth, she hit her first $10,000 month. The coaching company she worked with even mailed her a shiny $10K trophy. "I still have it on my shelf," she told me. "It reminds me that this is real, and I did it."

But her biggest transformation wasn't strategy. It was identity. She had to let go of the belief that she was the only one who could sell her program. "I was convinced no one could sell it like I could," she said. "But when I had a baby, I literally didn't have the time anymore. So I hired someone to do it. And guess what? It worked!" Almost immediately, she saw that the quality of her business wasn't tied to her ability to do everything alone. It grew when she trusted others.

Over time, she hired a full-time assistant, delegated client delivery, and eventually built a team of coaches and sales reps. Today, she no longer coaches clients one-on-one. And her clients are getting better results than ever. "Clients don't care if it's me personally—as long as they get the results. And often, my team delivers those results more consistently than I ever could."

Today, Anni's business consistently brings in numbers she once thought were impossible. Two months in a row, her team sold sixteen clients each month—$46,400 total revenue. And it didn't come from a viral post or a lucky surge. It came from systems. "We sell every week," she said. "That's the difference."

What impressed me most wasn't the money, but the life she built around it. During the early years with her child, she worked only three days a week, keeping Mondays and Fridays completely free. "Having that freedom to choose how I spend time with my baby was amazing. It's why I built this business in the first place." Even when she took maternity leave, the business kept running. Sales continued. Clients were supported. "That's the power of systems. That's freedom."

Even though she runs a $40K+ per month business, she doesn't work nights or weekends. Her schedule is light. Her team is strong. Her systems are solid. "Just because it's big doesn't mean it has to be hard. I work less than ever and the business runs better than ever."

What's interesting is that even now, with all her proof, she still sometimes struggles to see herself as the authority she clearly is. "Logically, I know I'm a leader in this space. But emotionally, I'm still catching up. I still don't fully see myself as 'the expert,' even though the results say otherwise." And yet, her consistency has made her a trusted voice in her niche—from YouTube to Instagram—without a single PR campaign or speaking tour.

Her growth is a direct reflection of everything this chapter teaches: sales as service, pricing with confidence, selling it yourself first, and then building the systems and team that allow the business to scale. "My revenue goal used to be $20,000/month. Now $50K feels natural. I still have doubts about hitting $100K months—but I know it's just a matter of time."

When I asked what she wants other women to know, she said: "You can charge premium prices even if you're just starting. Delegating doesn't reduce quality; it enhances it. You don't need to work 24/7 to build something great. And ease and ambition can co-exist if you build with intention."

How to Handle Objections

One of the most important parts of high-ticket sales is learning how to handle objections. The best approach is not by arguing or convincing, but by helping people think clearly. The goal is to guide someone to realize, on their own, that their hesitation is often just fear in disguise.

When objections come up after presenting the offer and price, I don't "handle" them in the traditional sense. Instead, I ask questions that help the person reflect on what's really holding them back.

For example, if they say, "I don't have the time," I ask: "How much time are you currently spending on things that don't actually move your business forward?"

If they say, "I can't afford it," I ask: "If you had a system that could consistently bring in high-paying clients, how quickly do you think this investment would pay itself back?"

If they say, "Now isn't the right time," I ask: "When do you think will be the right time to finally fix this problem, and what will have changed by then?"

These questions aren't tricks. They simply help the person step out of short-term thinking and into long-term perspective. When someone is about to make a meaningful investment, their brain naturally looks for safety—reasons to wait, stall, or play small. Your job is to help them see that waiting often carries a higher cost than moving forward.

The power of great objection handling is helping the client talk themselves into the decision.

How I Sell Today

When I think back to how we sold in the early days, the business looked very different. We operated in launch cycles—one big push every month. The cart would open for a few days, and we'd send emails, host webinars, and focus our energy on creating momentum during that short window. It worked well, but the problem was what came after. Once the launch ended, sales dropped too. For the rest of the month, we had nothing to sell.

Now we have an evergreen offer that brings in new clients day after day, week after week without the peaks and valleys of launch cycle. Our sales process runs continuously through content, lead nurturing, and consistent calls.

I still believe launches have their place, and we'll likely use them again for special campaigns or new programs. But the evergreen model has become the foundation of the business. It's calm, structured, and built to qualify clients before a single call ever happens.

Here's how it works:

Step 1: Lead generation. A potential client might come to us through a webinar, a social post, or an ad.

Step 2: Initial filter. From there, one of two things happens:

- *Self-application:* The lead books a call through our calendar and answers a few qualifying questions. If their answers show they aren't a fit, we cancel the call before it ever happens.
- *Appointment setter outreach:* Our appointment setter personally calls or messages the lead, asks those same questions, and only books them if they're ready and serious.

This means my sales team only speaks to *warm* or *hot* leads—people who have already raised their hand and shown genuine interest. By the time they're on the calendar, they're not being "sold to" in the traditional sense. They're looking for a solution and ready to invest in one.

That pre-qualification also makes it possible for us to offer commission-only roles. My salespeople aren't cold-calling strangers; they're having meaningful conversations with people who've already said, "I want help."

When a prospect gets on the call, we follow a structured script. It's not about pushing them into a decision. It's about guiding them through a series of questions:

- What are you struggling with right now?
- Why hasn't this problem been solved yet?
- What would it mean to you if this were fixed?

The goal is to help them clearly articulate what they already know deep down: They can't do it alone, they want to move faster, and they're ready for change. That's the moment we step in and say, "Here's how we can help you get from where you are to where you want to go."

This process is especially important when you're selling at a premium price point—$5,000, $10,000, or more. At this level, you don't need every prospect to say yes. A 20 percent close rate is healthy. If you're hitting 30 percent or more, you're performing exceptionally well. What matters most is that the right people are on the call in the first place.

One of the biggest upgrades we've made is having a live appointment setter call every lead. In the past, we relied on emails and messages. It worked okay, but it didn't have the same effect. The moment we added a real human voice—a team member personally reaching out—we elevated the experience. From that very first touchpoint, prospects felt seen, heard, and valued.

The numbers prove it. In Finland, our answer and show-up rates are around 90 percent, which is extraordinary compared to U.S. standards, where even 50 percent is considered strong. That difference is proof that calling works. While messages can often get ignored, a phone call builds connection. It shows prospects this isn't just a transaction—it's the start of a relationship.

Looking at how we sell today, it's clear how far we've come. We went from scrambling to close quick wins to running a refined, predictable system that serves both us and our clients. And that's the heart of this chapter: Sales isn't about chasing anyone or everyone. It's about building a process that respects your time, honors your clients, and creates a steady path for growth—one conversation at a time.

Key Takeaways

#1. Sales is service, not pressure.

Sales isn't about convincing or pushing; it's about guiding people toward the transformation they're already seeking. When you frame sales as helping someone take action on their goals, every conversation becomes a win-win.

#2. You must sell it yourself first.
Before you can delegate sales, you need to prove the offer works in your own hands. Running the first ten to fifteen calls yourself gives you the insights, confidence, and clarity to build a repeatable process others can follow.

#3. Confidence comes from proof.
Confidence isn't something you wait for—it's something you build. Each call, each client win, and each result is evidence that reinforces your belief in your offer and in yourself.

#4. Price with belief, not fear.
The price you charge reflects your conviction in the value you deliver. If you don't believe in your own price, no one else will either. Set a number you can stand behind, and lead the conversation with certainty.

#5. A strong process beats one-time tactics.
Premium sales don't happen by accident. Pre-qualifying leads, structuring calls, and adding personal touches like live outreach create a sales system that's consistent, scalable, and respectful to everyone involved.

Strategies & Tools
These tools will help you turn sales from something overwhelming into a clear, repeatable process. Think of them as the building blocks for selling with confidence—whether you're still doing all the calls yourself or starting to build a team.

The Discovery Call Framework
One of the most powerful tools you can have in sales is a *discovery framework*—a simple structure that helps you lead conversations with confidence. Instead of winging it or jumping into a pitch too soon, this framework keeps you focused on listening and understanding before you ever talk about your offer.

Here's how to use it:

1. **Set up a template for note taking.** Create this framework into a document or CRM so you can take notes while you talk. Make a new page for each prospect, and fill it out in real time.
2. **Guide the conversation.** Your goal is to gather the right information and help the prospect clarify their own challenges and desires. Here's what to cover:

   - **Motivation:** Why are they on this call now? What sparked their interest?
   - **Background:** What's their business or current situation?
   - **Current Challenges:** What problems are they facing, and why haven't they solved them yet?
   - **Desired Outcome:** What does success look like for them?
   - **Timeline:** Where do they want to be in three, six, or twelve months? (Match this to your program length, if applicable.)
   - **Why Now?:** Ask why this is important to them personally, and why it matters right now.

3. **Listen more than you speak.** The best sales calls feel like coaching sessions. When someone hears themselves saying out loud why they need help, they're already halfway to saying yes.
4. **Present the offer naturally.** Once you fully understand why they need your help and can clearly see your service as the bridge between where they are and where they want to go, you can transition to your offer. At this point, it won't feel pushy—it will feel like the obvious next step.

As you use this framework, remember that confident selling comes from clarity. If a prospect still sounds uncertain or hesitant, don't rush into a pitch. Keep asking questions until their problem is clear to you. If it becomes obvious they aren't ready, end the call without making an offer.

Always prioritize fit over closing. It's tempting to say yes to anyone willing to pay, especially early on, but bringing in the wrong clients will cost you far more in the long run. It's better to walk away than to spend months dealing with misaligned expectations.

Finally, notice how you feel during the conversation. If you catch yourself defending your price or talking in circles to justify the value, that's a red flag. It usually means the prospect isn't fully convinced yet. Instead of pushing harder, return to discovery and ask more questions.

When you approach sales this way, prospects feel seen and understood, and you leave the call knowing with confidence whether they're the right fit. If they are, enrolling them becomes a natural, collaborative next step rather than a pressured decision.

Lead Tracker (CRM)

Once you start having consistent sales conversations, you need a system to track what happens on those calls. This is where a *CRM (Customer Relationship Management)* tool comes in. Think of it as a home base for all your leads—a way to track every conversation and every relationship over time.

A CRM is important for many reasons. First of all, people don't always buy right away. Someone might book a call today, decide it's not the right time, and then return a year later (often because of thoughtful, proactive follow-up from the sales team) ready to invest. Without a system, you'd lose track of that entire journey and start from scratch every time you talk to them. With a CRM in place, you can see exactly what happened and when, giving you valuable context for every conversation.

Over time, this tracking reveals patterns. You'll start to notice which objections come up most often, where your best leads are coming from, and how long it typically takes someone to move from first contact to becoming a client. These insights allow you to refine both your marketing and your sales process, creating a smoother, more predictable path to growth.

What to include in your tracker:

- Name of the lead
- Source (ad, referral, social media, webinar, etc.)
- Outcome (Did they buy?)
- Revenue (cash collected on the call, total value of the sale)
- Objections (e.g., "no money," "wrong timing," etc.)
- Emotions/notes from the call (what stood out, tone, energy)
- Call summary (key takeaways)
- Recording link (if you save call recordings)

The benefit is twofold. First, it brings clarity for you as the founder. With a complete record of every interaction, you'll know exactly why people are saying yes—or no. That insight helps you refine your sales process, adjust your messaging, and improve over time.

Second, it creates consistency for your team. As your business grows, every salesperson can log calls in the same way, using the same system. This makes it easier to coach your team, review performance, and keep everyone centered around shared goals. Instead of scattered notes and guesswork, you have a single source of truth that supports growth and accountability.

Final Thoughts

Sales is the heartbeat of your business. It's what turns interest into action and allows your company to grow. In the early days, that heartbeat comes from you—the founder—showing up with confidence, serving your clients, and refining your offer one conversation at a time.

As you've seen throughout this chapter, mastering sales isn't just about scripts and systems; it's about becoming someone who knows how to lead others through transformation. When you believe in the value of what you're offering, you naturally create a safe, trustworthy space for clients to believe too.

Over time, as your systems grow and your team expands, sales becomes scalable. But even then, it never stops being personal. Every number on a spreadsheet represents a human being making a decision to change their life or business through your work. When you hold that perspective, sales becomes more than a skill—it becomes a service.

In the next chapter, we'll explore how to position yourself as the trusted authority people want to buy from. Because when prospects already see you as the expert, sales conversations become smoother, shorter, and more natural. Sales may bring revenue, but personal branding and PR bring reputation—and together, they form the foundation for sustainable growth.

CHAPTER 8
PERSONAL BRANDING AND PR—BECOMING THE AUTHORITY

A personal brand is what people say about you when you're not in the room.

And for that to even happen, you need people—clients, results, and proof of the transformation you deliver. Without that foundation, no PR push or brand strategist can manufacture a reputation that sticks. You can hire someone to design the perfect logo or craft polished messaging, but if you don't truly know the people you serve—or the impact you create in their lives—your brand is just decoration.

That's why the order matters. First, you do the groundwork. You serve clients. You deliver results. Then, over time, your brand naturally forms around that experience.

The problem is, most people get stuck chasing the wrong things. They obsess over the aesthetics, the curated Instagram feed, the polished website. They believe the secret is *more*—more followers, more likes, more subscribers.

But that's wrong.

You already have a brand before your website ever goes live. And no shiny redesign can fix a weak reputation.

What really matters isn't how many people are watching you, it's *who* you're reaching and whether your message moves them to act. You don't need to be everywhere or appeal to everyone. You need credibility, results, and a story that resonates with the right people.

In this chapter, we'll explore how to build a brand rooted in trust and impact—one that grows from real relationships and authentic authority, not smoke and mirrors. You'll learn how to position yourself as the go-to expert, create content that drives action, and attract opportunities that expand your reach in a sustainable way.

Building My Brand

I started building a personal brand long before it was even called that.

More than fifteen years ago now, I launched my first blog. Back then, blogging was one of the earliest ways to share your voice and build an online presence. I experimented with social media, sponsorships, and collaborations, testing ideas and learning how visibility could be leveraged, even monetized, long before I had the capital to invest in other parts of my business.

That early experience taught me something important: Media attention matters, but only when it's backed by results.

When I published my first book in 2021, I got my first taste of traditional PR. My publisher secured a few interviews and features, which felt exciting, but at the time, I didn't realize that pitching to the media was something I could do, so I didn't.

It wasn't until the following year, after I'd shifted to my new premium offer, that I began to understand the value of media exposure. By then, I also had a friend who specialized in helping entrepreneurs land press coverage, but I made the conscious decision to wait. I wanted to focus first on building the new program and getting real results for clients. I didn't just want visibility for visibility's sake. I wanted credibility. I wanted to know that when someone saw my name in a headline, there would be proof behind it.

There are plenty of PR coaches who teach people how to "get featured," but at the end of the day I've learned that real authority comes from client outcomes, not clever pitches. Once I had those results, I hired support to help me share them more widely. By 2023, I started landing interviews and features organically, and the media began to come to me rather than the other way around.

One of my biggest features—a spread in the top financial magazine in Finland—came directly from a single Facebook group post that went viral.

That post sparked attention from potential clients and even caught the eye of journalists, all because I had shown up consistently over time. But just like I mentioned in chapter 6 when dealing with trolls, visibility has a price. Alongside my exposure to the world came waves of criticism, skepticism, and even outright hate.

The first real wave came when I launched my beta program. The price point—$2,000—was unheard of in my space at the time, and to many outsiders, it automatically signaled "scam." It wasn't just the price, though. When I shared client wins, the results sounded unbelievable to people who had never experienced transformation at that level. Even today, when I post about success stories, I always get comments like, "This can't be real" or "You must be faking this."

And criticism didn't only come from strangers. Around that same time, I closed a couple on a sales call even though I knew deep down they weren't my ideal clients. I let my skills as a closer override my intuition, and it came back to bite me. The woman later began posting vague but damaging complaints in public groups. It escalated to the point where a lawyer sent me a letter, and I had to hire my own attorney. Thankfully, nothing came of it legally—we had clear agreements in place—but the emotional toll was enormous.

This period marked the beginning of my journey in learning how to handle public criticism. As you know from the stages I shared earlier when dealing with trolls, the first stage is always shock. I remember one day seeing a flood of nasty comments online and leaving for a lash appointment immediately afterward. I was so shaken that I walked in the wrong direction and missed the train station completely. When I finally arrived at my appointment, I lay there for two hours, heart racing, convinced I was going to die from the stress.

Then came avoidance. I kept posting because I had to—my clients were watching me, and I needed to model resilience—but I refused to read the comments. Meanwhile, the negativity grew louder, especially when a social media "critic" with a large following began targeting me publicly. The anxiety became overwhelming.

The final stage was acceptance. I began to see the patterns: Engagement, even negative engagement, boosted visibility. Journalists started calling me not *despite* the controversy, but *because of it*. Slowly, I realized that resistance wasn't always a bad thing—it often meant I was standing out, disrupting old ways of thinking, and offering something bold enough to challenge people's assumptions.

Over time, I even began responding directly to negative comments. By showing up with calmness and clarity, I disarmed critics and earned the respect of silent onlookers. By 2023, after returning from that much-needed trip to Portugal, I was no longer fazed by hate. I saw it as part of the territory that comes with leadership and visibility.

Looking back, that chapter of my journey taught me two powerful lessons that continue to shape my approach to branding today:

1. **Not everyone is your client.** If you push to close someone who isn't truly a fit, it will cost you far more than money.
2. **Hate is often just resistance.** People project their fears and insecurities onto what they don't understand—or what they don't believe is possible for themselves.

A coach once told me, "When you start hitting $100,000 months, the volume of clients grows and so does the likelihood of attracting difficult ones." That insight reframed the way I saw my challenges. It wasn't failure. It was simply a sign that I had stepped onto a bigger playing field.

Today, people admire the fact that I've stayed consistent year after year, no matter what has been said about me. That consistency has become part of my personal brand. It signals to my audience—and to the media—that I believe deeply in what I teach.

In addition to my authority being built on results, it was also built on the courage to keep showing up, telling the truth, and serving clients even when it's uncomfortable. That resilience, combined with client success stories, has done more for my personal brand than any logo or website ever could.

The Role of Authority

When it comes to building a personal brand, authority is everything.

Would you rather have the most beautiful website in your industry, or the strongest reputation for delivering actual results? Which one do you think will grow your business faster?

Results are the foundation of your brand. They are what prove that what you teach or offer actually works. Without them, no amount of branding or PR can create lasting credibility.

Your first priority should be getting results—for yourself and for your clients. When people see real transformation, numbers that matter, and stories they can relate to, your authority grows naturally. No fancy branding can replace that proof.

This also changes how you approach consistency. If you're constantly trying to "fake it till you make it," showing up online will feel exhausting because you're performing an identity you haven't fully earned. But when your authority is built on real wins, showing up feels authentic and effortless. You're simply sharing the truth of what you've already achieved.

Authority is also about what happens behind the scenes. Your *reputation*—how people experience you and your business—is the real measure of your brand. Leila Hormozi says it best: "Your personal brand is just your reputation."

If your client onboarding is broken, if your team isn't delivering, or if customers feel let down, no amount of sleek marketing will fix that. The whispers behind closed doors will shape your brand far more than anything you post online.

When I was scaling quickly, I learned this the hard way. I made a few bad hires, and those decisions caused ripple effects for nearly a year. Client issues piled up. It wasn't glamorous work, but fixing those problems—training the team, strengthening systems, taking full responsibility—was what actually strengthened my reputation long-term.

Authority also comes from preparation. Brené Brown once said something to me that completely reinforced this idea. I had the chance to ask her how she built such an incredible global platform with books, TV shows, and a deeply loyal audience. Her answer was simple but powerful: "Especially as a young woman, people will judge you, doubt you, and try to discredit you. That's why you need to be the most prepared person in the room. Authority comes from proof."

That advice applies to every entrepreneur. You don't need to be the smartest person in the room. You need to show up with more preparation than anyone else.

When you know your material inside and out, when you can clearly articulate your clients' struggles and how to solve them, your confidence radiates. Authority comes from that kind of readiness. It's not about using fancy jargon or flexing intelligence. It's about communicating complex ideas in a simple, relatable way.

And when you break down authority to its essentials, it really comes from four places:

1. Results: Get wins for yourself and your clients. Let proof do the talking.
2. Reputation: Deliver an exceptional client experience, and protect your integrity.
3. Preparation: Be so prepared that your confidence is undeniable.
4. Communication: Share your knowledge in a way that connects and inspires action.

When you focus on these four areas, your authority grows naturally. You won't have to fight for attention or "look the part." You'll be the authority because you've done the work to earn it.

The Role of PR in Personal Branding

Public relations can be a powerful amplifier for your personal brand, but only if the foundation is solid first. Many entrepreneurs make the mistake of chasing PR too early, thinking a glossy feature or media mention will make them credible. The truth is, PR doesn't create authority; it showcases authority you've already built.

PR can take many forms—like being featured in a business magazine, sharing your story on a podcast, or contributing expert insights to online publications. These opportunities can be incredibly valuable once your business has traction and clear results to highlight. When done at the right time, PR helps you reach a wider audience, strengthen your positioning, and attract clients who already see you as credible before you ever speak to them.

Think of PR like a spotlight. It shines on what's already there. If you haven't delivered real results for your clients or built a reputation for excellence, the spotlight will only highlight the gaps. But if you've put in the work—creating wins for clients, refining your systems, and showing up consistently—PR can take that proof and broadcast it to a much wider audience.

When you're featured in a respected outlet, it usually opens opportunities you might never have had otherwise. For example, after some of my early articles were published, I started receiving podcast invitations. Hosts wanted to talk about my journey: being a pioneer in my space, navigating waves of public criticism, and staying deeply committed to my work. These conversations weren't focused on the challenges themselves, but on the resilience, consistency, and belief that kept me moving forward.

Each feature built on the last, creating a ripple effect. A single article might lead to a podcast interview, which then leads to another media request, which then connects you with an entirely new audience.

That's the real value of PR; it opens doors you can't always predict.

It's not always easy to measure PR's direct impact on revenue, but you'll notice the effects in other ways. Whenever a new feature goes live, we see a spike in attention. More people start following on social media, more names show up in our DMs, and more prospects reference a feature or appearance on sales calls. On every call, we ask, "How did you find us?" and many times, they'll name a specific article or podcast appearance.

Even if you can't tie every sale back to a single piece of PR, media exposure creates visibility, visibility creates connection, and connection feeds into your lead generation system. That's how PR supports a business. It helps you build a steady drumbeat of recognition so that when people see your name, they already associate it with authority and results.

The key is to see PR as an amplifier, not the starting point. If you've been steadily building results and credibility, PR will magnify that work and attract new audiences who are ready to engage with you. But without that foundation, media mentions will fall flat—or worse, they'll draw attention before you're ready to deliver at a higher level. That's why the sequence matters: results first, PR second.

Marianna's Story: From Single Mom to Sought-After Authority

When I think about the difference between "having a brand" and actually building authority, I think of Marianna.

When she joined our program, she was living in the Netherlands, technically unemployed, a single mother with a baby, and on temporary government support after a short maternity leave. Before that, she had spent years working in marketing and project management inside major hospitality brands—experience that gave her an insider's understanding of how teams function, how leaders communicate, and where performance breaks down. She didn't have a personal brand. She didn't have a following. She didn't have a big network or a polished website.

She'd dreamed of entrepreneurship for years, but it stayed in the realm of "someday." She believed she needed more qualifications, more time, more certainty. What she really needed was someone to say, "You can start now."

Like many experts, Marianna carried a whole backpack of assumptions about what had to be true before she could be taken seriously. She thought she needed to finish a coaching degree first. She thought she had to work for free to prove herself. She believed success in entrepreneurship had to be slow and hard—something you grind toward over years.

I told her she didn't need any of that.

Instead, she built a simple, premium offer for team leaders in the hospitality industry—focusing on leadership performance, communication, and emotional intelligence for frontline managers. The promise was clear: to help leaders run healthier teams and improve results without burning out. She started with one channel: LinkedIn. No website. No funnel. No brand colors. Just one focused piece of content and direct outreach to the right people.

"I had no website. I still don't. But I learned that one focused piece of content can be enough if your message is right."

Her first sales cycle was proof of that. She used the premium pilot method and booked five sales calls. Two of them said yes. And they weren't small accounts either; they were major companies, including names like Espresso House and Burger King. "That's when I realized this isn't just a dream. This is working," she said.

From the outside, it looked like things moved quickly. But under the surface, she was undoing years of conditioning. One of her biggest realizations was that her real fear wasn't failure—it was success. "What I really feared was: What if I actually succeed? What if this changes everything?" That's the kind of question that comes up when you're a solo parent with a baby on your hip and you're building a business that could transform your life.

Because of that, she was intentional from day one about how she built. She didn't want a business that required her to hustle 24/7. She wanted something sustainable—three focused days a week, with space for her daughter and life outside of work. So instead of trying to do everything herself to "prove" she could, she started asking different questions: "Where can I save time? Where can I buy support?"

She outsourced cleaning. She hired a bookkeeper. She used tools like LinkedIn Sales Navigator to make outreach more efficient. Later, she brought in a lead generation agency to support her pipeline. At the time of this writing, she's planning for her first assistant and thinking ahead to what a scalable team looks like for her business.

"I'm proud I've created this with kindness," she said. "I didn't burn out. I didn't hustle 24/7. I made space for joy, for my daughter, and still made it work."

That "kind" way of building has become part of her brand. Her style as a coach is grounded, strategic, and, well, human. She doesn't just talk about performance; she talks about the emotional reality of leadership. She tracks her clients' results from the very beginning, and every client she's worked with so far has wanted to renew. Even her early pilot offer—what she jokingly called "business therapy"—led to long-term partnerships.

"One client said, 'You believing in me made me believe in myself as a leader,'" she told me. "That changed how she showed up at work—and that's what this is about."

This is what I mean when I say your brand is built on proof. It didn't matter that Marianna didn't have a big online presence. What mattered was that the people she worked with transformed. Their teams shifted. Their leaders grew. And those results became the foundation of her authority.

Only after that did PR start to show up.

Marianna began getting featured in industry publications like *Aromi* magazine—a leading hospitality-trend publication across the Nordics. McDonald's Finland interviewed her as an example of post-McDonald's career success. None of that came from a PR agency pitching her as "the next big thing." It came because her results and story were interesting. She had gone from unemployed single mother on government support to trusted advisor for major hospitality brands—and she had built that path in a way that was calm, intentional, and effective.

What's more is Marianna doesn't see this visibility as vanity; she sees it as responsibility. "I want to be a role model for my daughter," she said. "I want her to grow up seeing what's possible." That's the deeper layer of authority—when your work isn't just about revenue or reputation, but about what it signals to the people watching you up close.

"In corporate life, I always saw life through a tunnel," she reflected.

"I knew exactly what was coming into my account each month—and exactly what wasn't. Now, the potential is limitless."

Her journey is a perfect illustration of what we've been talking about in this chapter. She didn't start with a large audience, a glossy brand, or a ready-made network. She started with clarity, one channel, and the willingness to charge premium prices from day one. The authority came from results. The reputation followed. And only then did PR become a natural extension of the brand she'd already built.

Her advice to other women standing on the edge of change is simple: "Don't listen to the ones who've never done what you dream of. Listen to the ones who have."

How to Handle Criticism

When you step into greater visibility, criticism is pretty much guaranteed. The more impact you make, the more people will have opinions about how you do it. At first, this can feel crushing. You've poured your heart into your work, and suddenly strangers are questioning your integrity, your methods, or even your character.

I've been there. In the beginning, the negative comments hit me like a tidal wave. They felt like a direct attack on who I was. Over time, though, I realized something important: Criticism is part of playing on a bigger field. The key is learning how to respond—or when not to respond at all.

Handling Negative Comments

At first, I believed the best approach was to ignore negativity completely. But now I see it differently. I don't respond to every troll, especially not to comments like, "This can't be real" or "This is a scam!" Those comments aren't coming from a place of genuine curiosity—they're meant to provoke.

But when someone raises a thoughtful objection, even if it's misinformed, I often respond. Not because I expect to change their mind—arguing online rarely works—but because my response is for everyone else watching silently. When you answer with grace, professionalism, and confidence, people notice. They see the troll's negativity, and they see your calm, measured reply. That contrast strengthens your credibility (and remember: The engagement boosts your algorithm, just like we discussed earlier).

For example, if someone comments, "That would never work in my industry," I'll reply with an example from one of my clients in their exact field. Instead of defending myself, I focus on adding value and clarifying the truth for the silent audience watching.

Dealing with Haters

Success and haters go hand in hand. The more you succeed, the more hate you'll get. The reality is, haters will always show up. And when they do, you have a choice: let them affect you, or don't and keep moving forward. These moments are tests. They challenge you to confront how deeply you believe in what you're building. I've seen many entrepreneurs quit at this stage—not because their business wasn't working, but because the pressure and criticism became too heavy to carry.

I've faced those moments myself, when it felt like the easiest path would be to give up. But each time, I reminded myself: *My vision is bigger than this one person.* So I kept going. One more day. One more week. One more year. And over time, I built resilience.

Today, very little rattles me because I've basically already heard it all at this point. The criticism hasn't disappeared (it never will) but my reaction to it has changed.

The Bigger Vision: Playing on a Bigger Field

Every single article written about me in the media has been positive—well, except one. But even that piece wasn't truly negative. It was simply a journalist doing their own "investigation" after being influenced by online critics. They didn't find anything shady, because there wasn't anything shady to find.

One of the biggest fears almost every entrepreneur carries is the fear of being canceled, misunderstood, or publicly attacked. And even if this fear comes true and it happens to you, you will still be okay. Your business can still grow. You can still sleep at night. The fear feels paralyzing in your mind, but in reality, it's survivable.

In Finland, some of our normal sales practices—like outreach messages or booking calls—are viewed as unconventional. But that doesn't make them wrong. It just means we're pioneering a model others haven't seen before. And pioneering always comes with pushback.

When I face criticism now, I remind myself of my bigger vision. I've always said I want to be like the Oprah of the business world—creating massive, global impact. And if that's the level I'm aiming for, of course there will be challenges along the way. Even Oprah gets sued, criticized, and questioned. Even top entrepreneurs like Alex and Leila Hormozi—one of the most influential business-building couples in the online education and scaling space—face public scrutiny, to the point that they need legal disclaimers on every video they release.

That's what it means to play on a bigger field. The spotlight is brighter, and so is the noise. But criticism and controversy doesn't mean you've failed; they're proof that you've reached a level where your work actually matters. So when hate comes my way, I see it as training for what's next. These moments are preparing me for an even bigger stage.

Anchoring Yourself in Proof and Support

In the hardest moments, what kept me grounded was proof.

While the hate was loud, I had a growing community of clients who believed in me. They were getting real results, and often, they'd step into the comments to defend me without me ever asking. It was amazing. Seeing clients publicly say, "This works. I've experienced it myself," reminded me of the bigger picture.

But human nature has a bias: we feel the sting of one negative comment far more than the warmth of ten positive ones. To balance that, my team and I began taking screenshots of every client win. We created a running "wall of proof" in our Slack channel as a daily reminder of the impact we were making. One client hit $18,000 in sales within her first two months of the program. Another surpassed her entire monthly target in just a few weeks. Another finally achieved consistent five-figure months and, for the first time, felt free from the constant stress of finding clients.

On hard days, I could scroll through those screenshots and remember the truth. The noise online didn't define me. The results did.

And it wasn't just about me anymore, it was about my team. They were in the trenches with me, supporting me, depending on me to keep showing up so the business could continue and their roles would remain secure. Surround yourself with the proof, with the clients who believe in you, and with the teammates who see the impact firsthand. That's how you stay strong when the outside noise gets loud.

Why Criticism Means You're Growing

The bottom line is criticism is a sign you're growing into the role of authority. When you're just starting out, no one cares enough to criticize you. It's only when you start making waves—when your message begins to matter—that people react. The louder the reaction, the more you know you're hitting a nerve.

So don't mistake criticism as a sign you're doing something wrong. See it for what it is: evidence that you're becoming the very authority you've been working so hard to be.

Family Reactions to Becoming an Authority

When you step into the spotlight as an entrepreneur, you expect strangers to have opinions. What you don't expect is how deeply your own family's reactions can affect you. For many of us, that's where the real challenge lies—not in the trolls online, but in the people sitting across from us at the dinner table.

When I was growing up, stability was important in my family. Most of my relatives have traditional jobs—nurses, teachers, engineers. They value security and predictability. So when I started my entrepreneurial journey, especially in such a visible way, it didn't fit their worldview.

The biggest tension was with my mom. She's always admired academic titles and authority figures like professors. So when I wrote a nonfiction book without a formal academic background, it was jarring for her. Suddenly, I was stepping into a position of authority that she didn't quite understand—or even believe in.

At first, her reactions cut deeper than any online criticism ever could. Trolls are easy to dismiss. But when it's your mom questioning you, or your partner asking if you should just get a "real job," the doubt seeps in. My mom even asked my sister to talk me out of posting on social media because she thought it was embarrassing.

Conversations with her about my work were rarely positive. She's never been quick to give praise, and instead of encouragement, I was met with criticism or silence. In the early days, when my results weren't visible yet, her disapproval made me question everything. There were moments when I thought, *Maybe she's right. Maybe I'm not capable. Maybe this isn't real.* Even after I started making money online, she couldn't see it—because it didn't look like work to her. She once suggested I apply for a job delivering mail, just so I'd have something tangible she could understand.

Over time, however, I began to realize that her reaction wasn't really about me. She had been a single mother, working multiple jobs—mail delivery, telemarketing, evening shifts—just to keep our family afloat. To her, stability was survival. Publicly sharing about my business wins, struggles, and money felt foreign to her, even shameful. In our family, you kept things private to avoid making others jealous. My openness online clashed with everything she believed.

There were painful moments. She once watched a livestreamed talk I gave and felt hurt by a story I told, even though I never named her. She saw herself in my words, which made her uncomfortable. I've come to understand that sometimes people see themselves in your growth—and that reflection can be hard for them to face.

Eventually, I had to accept that she might never fully understand or support my work. Today, we're still in contact, but our relationship has boundaries. I keep conversations neutral—updates about the kids, family news, safe topics. I no longer share the deeper parts of my business journey with her.

That decision gave me freedom. It meant I could still love her, still show up for family gatherings, without constantly reopening old wounds. I learned that you don't have to cut someone off completely, but you can limit how much of your heart you hand over if they keep responding with negativity.

The truth is, the real battle was never between my mom and me—it was inside myself. For so long, I journaled about wanting her approval, hoping she'd one day say she was proud of me. My early journal pages are filled with pep talks to myself, reminders to keep going even when she didn't believe in me. At the time, it felt like her disapproval was the thing holding me back. But eventually, I realized it wasn't her—it was me. *I* was the one giving her opinion so much power.

I then shifted my focus inward, rooting for myself even when she wouldn't.

Her discomfort is her story, not mine.

Evolving My Brand

Five years into the business, my approach to brand building looks completely different than it did in the early days. Back in 2022, during a wave of online hate, we did a major PR push. It helped to have those positive articles to point to—tangible proof I could show when critics questioned my legitimacy. But I quickly realized that sharing those links didn't actually change anyone's mind. If anything, it made the critics angrier. They saw it as me trying to prove myself. In the moment, the PR was valuable, but it wasn't true brand building.

Real brand building didn't begin until our fifth year, when we brought in a brand strategist to look at everything holistically: our website, logos, messaging, and overall direction. For the first time, we had a clear strategy, not just scattered press features. This shifted how I thought about my role as a leader and a public figure. I began sharing not just numbers and wins, but also more vulnerable and relatable stories that showed the human side of what I do.

A conversation in London recently reminded me why this matters so much. I met a young Finnish woman, just twenty years old, who told me she'd been following my journey since my Career Girl blogging days. Her father, a Nigerian man, had struggled deeply as an entrepreneur in Finland, and because of that, she felt hesitant to start her own business. But seeing me succeed made her believe it was possible for her too. That dinner stayed with me. It made me realize how important it is to share my journey openly—not just the polished highlights, but the real, human story behind the results. I've even started thinking about hosting small gatherings for young women, with no business agenda at all, just to inspire them. In the U.S., philanthropy is a natural part of entrepreneurship. For me, this feels like my own version of giving back, and it softens my brand in a way that balances out the hard edge of talking about money, success, and growth all the time.

We've also been pouring resources into long-term projects that won't bring an immediate return: this book, our YouTube channel, and other forms of deeper content creation. These efforts take time, money, and energy, but they build trust and depth. For example, when I mention to someone that I'm writing a book, their perception of me changes instantly. It positions me as someone who's committed to this work for the long haul—not just someone chasing the next quick win.

At the same time, we've refined our social media strategy across multiple platforms. Each one plays a different role. YouTube is where we focus on long-form, authentic storytelling. The goal isn't to go viral but to build deep trust by sharing what works, what doesn't, and what we've learned along the way. These videos tend to convert well because people can see the thoughtfulness and logic behind what we do. Instagram is more lifestyle and inspiration. It's lighter, more visual, and a place for connection. Facebook is now mostly for groups, where I can connect with smaller, niche communities and then funnel people over to Instagram or YouTube.

LinkedIn has been the biggest surprise. At the time of this writing, its algorithm works a lot like Facebook did years ago—it gives visibility to posts even if you don't have a massive following. I use LinkedIn to share market insights, reflections on the business landscape, and practical advice, like "Here's what you're doing wrong and how to fix it." I also make announcements there and run call-to-action posts that invite people to comment with a keyword to receive something valuable, like a free guide or webinar replay.

We're now working closely with a friend of mine who's a talent manager. She's helped other controversial public figures in Finland evolve their brands into something bigger and more sustainable. Her advice has been clear: Balance the high-achiever content with softness and vulnerability. In the past, I focused heavily on results and performance—numbers, proof, wins. While that's all real, people only see what you put in front of them. From the outside, it can start to look perfect, almost untouchable. Sharing mistakes and lessons learned has always been part of my story, but now we're making sure that side doesn't get buried under the highlight reel.

That's the strategy moving forward: a more complete picture—one that shows resilience and results while also revealing humanity and relatability.

Key Takeaways

#1. **Results before recognition.**
True authority doesn't come from a polished logo, a beautiful website, or a viral post. It comes from getting real results for your clients. Serve first, create impact, and let those outcomes build your reputation.

#2. **Media amplifies; it doesn't create.**
PR and media features are powerful tools, but they can't manufacture credibility. They work best when they highlight the results and reputation you've already built through consistent, meaningful work.

#3. Criticism is a sign of growth.
The more visible you become, the more criticism you'll face. Haters are proof you're expanding into new territory. Respond with professionalism, focus on the silent majority watching, and keep moving forward.

#4. Family may not understand—and that's okay.
Sometimes the hardest resistance comes from the people closest to you. Their reactions come from their own fears and stories, not your worth or vision. Root for yourself even when they can't.

#5. Consistency builds trust over time.
Lasting authority is built through steady action. Keep showing up, sharing wins and lessons, and letting your audience see the full picture of who you are—not just the highlight reel. Over time, consistency itself becomes proof of your credibility.

Strategies & Tools

Now that you've built real authority through your results, it's time to share that story with a wider audience. The following strategies will help you turn credibility into visibility—and visibility into long-term momentum. You'll learn how to pitch yourself to the media, craft a clear brand story that journalists and podcast hosts can connect with, and make the most of every feature you land. These are practical, repeatable tools designed to help your expertise reach more people, strengthen your reputation, and create steady opportunities for growth.

Pitch Yourself to the Media

Did you know that you don't have to wait to be discovered? You can pitch yourself to the media. Many experts assume journalists will somehow find them, but the best opportunities often come from simply reaching out with a clear, relevant idea.

PR doesn't have to be complicated. A short, well-angled email is often all it takes to get noticed. Instead of asking to be featured, think like a journalist. Lead with a potential headline that would catch their attention, such as:

- "Former teacher turned coach reveals why most experts never scale."
- "Are Finnish entrepreneurs pricing themselves out of success?"

Then write one paragraph explaining why it matters now, how it connects to your work, and what perspective or data you can offer. The best pitches link your personal experience to a broader theme—something that helps the journalist tell a story their readers will care about.

When it comes to PR, visibility only matters if you have a system behind it. As Daniel Priestley says, attention disappears like rain in the desert unless you've built channels to capture it. Every time your name appears in an article, podcast, or interview, there should be a clear next step for people who discover you. Maybe that's a free resource, a newsletter, or a deeper program. That's how visibility turns into relationships instead of one-off moments.

You don't need a PR agency to make this happen either. You just need:

- a clear angle or insight that stands out,
- a short, journalist-style email that offers a story idea, and
- the consistency to follow up once or twice if you don't hear back.

Journalists' contact details are often listed in their articles, usually near the top or bottom. If not, reach out via LinkedIn with a short message introducing your idea. And if you're feeling bold and want to stand out, call them. Journalists receive hundreds of emails, so a brief, polite call can make a lasting impression.

Craft Your Brand Story for Media

Before you pitch yourself to any media, take ten to fifteen minutes to write down your answers to the following prompts. These help you find the "story hook"—the angle that makes your experience newsworthy or relevant. These prompts will help you turn your background into a clear, media-ready narrative:

1. **Origin:** Where did your journey begin? What problem, insight, or turning point made you start your business?
2. **Shift:** What changed—in you, in your industry, or in the world—that made your work necessary or timely?
3. **Mission:** What are you trying to change or challenge through your business or message?
4. **Proof:** What evidence or results show that your approach works? (Client success, data, or personal transformation.)
5. **Relevance:** Why does this matter now? What current conversation, trend, or tension makes your story important today?

Once you've answered these questions, you'll have the foundation for your first pitch email or LinkedIn message. Keep it short and specific with one paragraph that shows who you are, what you've achieved, and why your story fits today's headlines. For example:

"Hi [Name], I've noticed you've written about [topic]. I recently [insert proof/result] helping [type of people] with [pain/shift]. I believe this reflects a bigger trend: [insert relevance]. Would you be open to a short chat to see if this could fit your upcoming coverage?"

Pro tip: Keep it human and current. Avoid generic language, and focus on real people, real change, and real timing. If you can describe your brand story in a single paragraph that would fit in a journalist's inbox, you're ready to start pitching.

Make the Most of Your Media Wins

Once your stories start getting published or your interviews go live, your job isn't over—it's just beginning. Media exposure only creates real momentum if you use it well.

Make sure your systems can handle the attention. A single feature can bring in a surge of traffic, messages, or new followers. Have a process for where those people go next, whether that's a lead magnet, an email sequence, a DM workflow, or a call funnel. Visibility should amplify a system that's already working. The media is fuel, not the foundation.

When you land a feature, like an article, podcast, or interview, share it widely. Post it on social media, include it in your newsletter, and repurpose the best quotes or insights into new content. A single piece of coverage can become weeks of authority-building posts if you use it intentionally.

Finally, track your outreach and coverage. A simple spreadsheet works:

- Column 1: Outlet, journalist, or podcast name
- Column 2: Date you pitched
- Column 3: What you sent
- Column 4: Follow-up date
- Column 5: Result (response, booked, published)

Staying organized helps you build relationships with journalists and ensures no opportunity slips through the cracks. Media coverage compounds. One feature leads to another, and soon you're seen as the go-to voice in your niche. With the right systems, every piece of visibility becomes a building block for lasting authority.

Final Thoughts

Building a personal brand isn't about being everywhere or pleasing everyone. It's about being intentional—choosing to show up consistently, standing firmly in your results, and letting your reputation grow from the impact you create.

The strongest brands aren't built on perfect logos or flashy websites. They're built on trust. And trust comes from two things: delivering real results and communicating those results in a way that connects with the right people. When you focus on results first, the credibility follows. When you have credibility, PR and media features amplify your message instead of creating noise.

Along the way, you'll face challenges—criticism, misunderstandings, even resistance from those closest to you. These moments aren't signs to stop; they're proof that you're stepping into true authority. Visibility always comes with opinions, but how you respond to them determines how far you'll go.

As you move forward, remember this: Visibility is only as powerful as the client experience behind it.

In the next chapter, we'll explore how to create sustainable success—designing a business that not only delivers results today but also scales with you, giving you the freedom to lead, grow, and thrive for years to come.

CHAPTER 9

SUSTAINABLE SUCCESS— BUILDING A BUSINESS THAT SCALES FOR YOU

"Do you actually want to scale?" my mentor asked me back in 2022. "Do you even understand what scaling means?"

At the time, I thought scaling just meant rapid growth—more money, more clients, more success. It sounded exciting, like a straight path to the next big breakthrough. What I didn't realize was that true scaling isn't about speed. It's about creating streamlined, repeatable systems that allow you to serve more people without burning out or sacrificing quality.

The online business world often markets "scaling" as a quick win: flashy launches, temporary revenue spikes, and numbers that look impressive on social media. But without a strong foundation, those wins crumble under pressure.

That's why, after a year of massive growth back in 2022, I made a counterintuitive decision to slow down. For the next two years, we didn't chase new offers or aggressive expansion. Instead, we focused on fixing the cracks and building a structure strong enough to grow on.

It wasn't glamorous. In fact, from the outside, it looked boring— no viral campaigns, no headline-worthy launches. But it was necessary. Because when you scale a shaky foundation, you don't just scale revenue—you scale problems.

What made this season even more challenging was the internal battle happening behind the scenes. For the ego, this kind of slow, steady rebuilding is hard. When you live in an industry obsessed with speed and shiny numbers, you're constantly fighting the urge to chase quick growth—especially when you know that pressure comes from the outside, not from within. It's easy to feel like you're falling behind when everyone around you seems to be "winning" faster.

This is where Simon Sinek's concept of the finite versus infinite game became a powerful anchor for me. So many entrepreneurs are playing the finite game: chasing short-term wins, obsessing over how they compare to others, and trying to "get ahead" in an imaginary race. But scaling sustainably requires a different mindset: the infinite game. It's a long-term mission, guided by a bigger vision and a commitment to building something that lasts beyond the next launch or the next revenue milestone.

When you remember that you're playing the infinite game, slowing down to strengthen your foundation doesn't feel like falling behind. It feels like leadership. It feels like maturity. It feels like choosing your future self (and your future business) over the temporary validation of fast growth.

In this chapter, we'll explore what it really takes to scale sustainably, so your business grows stronger with every breakthrough.

The Paradox of Scaling

There's a belief that scaling begins with automation, systems, or hiring. But in reality, almost every scalable business starts with the founder doing intensely unscalable work.

This is the part most people never talk about. The hours spent serving clients one by one. The personal conversations. The manual problem-solving. It's the messy middle where nothing is leveraged yet, but everything important is being learned.

I've seen this pattern in my own journey, and it shows up again and again in the stories of the most successful founders in the world. Mark Zuckerberg didn't scale Facebook by sitting behind a laptop. He went to campus after campus, talking to students in person and convincing them to sign up. Whitney Wolfe Herd, the founder of Bumble, literally walked into college sororities and spoke to women directly, one group at a time, persuading them to download and trust the app. Sarah Blakely used to visit department stores and personally rearrange her Spanx displays to make sure customers actually noticed her product.

None of that was scalable. But all of it was essential.

Those early, unglamorous actions gave them the data, feedback, and conviction they needed to build systems that eventually scaled to millions. The same principle applies to expert entrepreneurs. Before you hire, automate, or delegate, you need to be in the trenches with your clients. You learn what works by doing it yourself. You refine your message by hearing real objections. You validate your offer by delivering results over and over again.

That's the paradox of scaling: The systems that eventually free you can only be built after you've done the work that doesn't scale. The unscalable work is where clarity comes from, where confidence comes from, and where the real foundation for growth is formed.

Every founder wants scalability, but the ones who actually get there are the ones who aren't afraid to start with the work no one else sees.

Scaling the Right Way

Once you've done the work that doesn't scale, you're finally in a position to think about scaling the right way. But before you do, it's important to be clear about what scaling actually means and what it doesn't.

In general, we think of growth in linear terms: You add more resources (capital, people, or technology), and revenue increases as a result. But that's not the true definition of scaling. Scaling is when revenue increases *without* a substantial increase in resources. It isn't just about chasing bigger numbers or growing as fast as possible. True scaling is about building a business that can grow without requiring more and more of your personal time and energy. It's creating a machine that continues to run and expand, even when you're not the one pushing every lever.

The path to scaling happens in stages. First, you need a product-market fit. This is where you nail down your core offer—the program or service that people truly want and are willing to pay for month after month. Without this, no amount of marketing or hiring will fix the underlying problem.

Once you've proven your offer works and clients are getting consistent results, you enter the second stage: organizing and systemizing. This is where you step back and start creating processes that make your business run smoothly. It means documenting standard operating procedures, streamlining workflows, and solving recurring problems at the root. Think of this stage like strengthening the foundation of a house. If you don't fix the cracks now, every new level you add will make them worse.

Only after you've completed these first two stages are you ready for the third: scaling with people. This is where you bring in team members to run the systems you've built, freeing you from being the bottleneck. Scaling through people allows you to grow without burning out, but it only works if the systems are strong and clear.

If you skip straight to hiring without first proving your offer and refining your processes, you'll create chaos instead of growth. That's why timing matters. Scaling is not a single event either—it's a series of deliberate steps. Done right, it sets you up for long-term success. Done too soon, it can unravel everything you've worked so hard to build.

And even when you are ready, scaling won't always feel smooth or easy. There will still be moments of doubt, sleepless nights, and uncomfortable decisions. But when you've built the right foundation, you can lean on your systems and team with confidence, knowing your business is strong enough to support the growth ahead.

At the end of the day, sustainable growth comes down to two things: systems and data.

It's not about chasing every new idea or throwing together a fresh campaign each week based on a gut feeling. That kind of growth is reactive, not sustainable. A business that truly scales runs on systems—systems that are tracked, measured, and constantly improved.

The key is to let the data guide your decisions. When something doesn't work, ask questions like, "What does the system need to do differently?" From there, you refine, optimize, and keep building.

That's how you create a business that grows predictably and sustainably—one where success isn't a surprise, but the natural outcome of strong systems fueled by data.

My "Problem-Solving" Years

Back in 2022, while our revenue jumped by over 1,000 percent, our systems didn't grow with it. We were adding clients at a rapid rate, yet we didn't have consistent processes to support them. Every new sale put more strain on the team, and the cracks began to show. Some days, it felt like I was holding the whole business together with duct tape and sheer willpower.

The first thing we addressed was client delivery. Every client success manager had their own way of operating, which meant inconsistent results. To fix that, we created a clear delivery playbook so every client received the same level of care and outcomes, no matter who was supporting them.

Next, we strengthened team leadership. Even though we already had KPIs, roles, and check-ins, I didn't yet have the skills or confidence to run those systems well. Over time, our one-on-ones became more structured, our metrics clearer, and our team communication more effective.

Then came marketing and sales where we shifted away from depending on one campaign or channel. The market was changing, so we built a diversified ecosytem—YouTube, Instagram, LinkedIn—creating stability rather than relying on quick wins.

On the operations and admin side, we streamlined everything. We documented how to handle client wins, standardized processes for dealing with unhappy clients, and made sure no one on the team needed to be handheld through daily tasks.

And finally, brand building: We started hosting large events in Finland, partnering as sponsors with others, and intentionally raising our visibility—not just online, but in person.

From the outside, it may have looked like we were standing still with revenue staying steady, hovering between $750,000 and $800,000 annually. But inside the company, we were setting the foundation. Instead of scaling chaos, we were building processes designed for a $10 million business. So when the time came to step back into growth mode, we didn't just grow faster—we grew *better*.

Scaling Is About Making Bets

Scaling isn't a straight path—it's a series of decisions made with incomplete information. Every hire you make, every ad campaign you run, every structural change to your offer is essentially a bet. You're investing resources today with the belief that they'll pay off tomorrow.

The challenge is that growth always takes more time, money, and energy than you think it will. It's never as clean or predictable as you hope. You might project a certain revenue number by year's end, only to find yourself solving unexpected problems instead of sprinting ahead. That's normal. Scaling comes in cycles: You grow, you encounter new bottlenecks, you fix them, and only then can you grow again.

One of the biggest bets you'll face is around pricing. Raising your rates can feel terrifying because it often creates an immediate dip in sales. When that happens, it's tempting to panic and lower your price again just to fill spots. But that quick fix doesn't address the real issue.

I've been through this myself. When we raised our prices, there was a period where sales slowed down. I knew some prospects would have said yes at the old rate, and part of me wanted to backtrack. But I held firm. I reminded myself that I wasn't just selling a program; I was building a business at a higher level.

When you commit to a premium price point, you also commit to upgrading everything around it: your messaging, your marketing, and even the client experience. That's the hard part. It forces you to get sharper in the marketing and more precise with your sales process.

Many entrepreneurs get stuck here. They raise prices once, see a temporary slowdown, and immediately retreat. But if you stay the course, you begin attracting more committed, higher-quality clients who are a better fit for your program. Those clients then get better results and create fewer headaches for you and your team.

Every time you hold your ground at a new level, you grow into it. That process builds the resilience and clarity you need to scale sustainably. While scaling usually results in bigger numbers, scaling also necessitates becoming the kind of leader whose systems, team, and vision can support those numbers without breaking.

That's why I say scaling is a series of bets. Some will pay off quickly. Others will test your patience. But if you keep refining, learning, and staying committed, those bets compound, and that's when true, sustainable growth begins.

My Bigger Bets

At the end of 2024, after those two steady years, I made the decision to scale—not just to grow revenue, but to evolve as a leader and entrepreneur. Scaling meant betting on myself all over again, investing in areas that wouldn't bring immediate returns but were crucial for long-term growth.

Some of those bets felt exciting, like writing this book or developing a stronger YouTube strategy. Others were less glamorous, like refining systems or restructuring the team. And some bets didn't pay off right away.

For instance, I spent six months trying one YouTube approach only to realize it wasn't producing results. Instead of holding on just because of the time and money invested, I pivoted. I brought in a new coach, adjusted my content strategy, and kept moving forward.

That's the nature of scaling: The strategies that get you to one level won't take you to the next. If I had clung to what worked before, I might have kept seeing small, incremental growth. But true scaling requires making bold, sometimes uncomfortable decisions—building the team before you feel ready, investing in new channels, and moving quickly when something isn't working.

A concept that shaped my thinking on this came from Peter Hinssen's talk at the Nordic Business Forum in 2025. He explained that most leaders spend their time fixing yesterday's problems or managing today's tasks. Some even plan for tomorrow. But the people who build enduring companies carve out deliberate time to design what he calls the "Day After Tomorrow." This is the chapter that hasn't arrived yet, the version of your business that doesn't exist yet.

If you wait until you reach the top to plan your next move, you're already behind. Thinking ahead—before you're forced to—keeps you adaptable, strategic, and ready for the next evolution of your company.

So in 2025, my focus was on building the right team to support our next stage of growth. I ran recruitment campaigns, interviewed dozens of candidates, and strengthened our fulfillment side so the business doesn't rely solely on me.

One of the biggest bets I made was promoting Saana as the operations manager. It was a huge leap, not only financially—since I offered her double the salary she'd earned before—but also in terms of trust. I knew that if this hire worked out, it would free me to focus on leadership instead of micromanaging daily operations. Thankfully, that bet paid off. She has been instrumental in stabilizing and scaling our company, and it remains one of the best decisions I've ever made.

Of course, not every bet works out. I'd had a failed experience with a previous operations manager, and while that was difficult at the time, it turned out to be a gift in hindsight. That failure taught me exactly what I didn't want and sharpened my instincts for the next hire. That's the beauty of experience; it makes your future bets wiser.

And when something doesn't work, I don't dwell on it. Energy spent on self-blame is energy stolen from problem-solving.

Take our two failed attempts at running an English-language webinar. The first time, a glitch in the automation meant participants couldn't even find the event. Oops! The second time, a mix-up in the landing pages promoted two different time slots. Both times, turnout was embarrassingly low.

Was it frustrating? Absolutely. But instead of pointing fingers or spiraling into shame, I simply said, "Okay, this can't happen again. Let's fix it and move on."

Look at each bet as a hypothesis: Maybe this will work; maybe it won't. What matters is committing fully while you test and then adjusting quickly when the data tells you it's not working. Something I've noticed again and again—both in my business and in my clients' results—is that success often comes down to the number of attempts. Most people test something a handful of times and assume it "didn't work." But there's a huge difference between trying something ten times and trying it a thousand times. Extraordinary results almost always come from extraordinary persistence.

For me, these bets have shown up in different areas of the business:

- **Pricing:** Raising our rates was a leap of faith. I didn't know if clients would say yes, but holding firm gave us higher-quality clients and better results.
- **YouTube:** As mentioned, the first approach failed, so I pivoted, hired a coach, and rebuilt our content strategy. And the reason I keep trying is because I know YouTube will eventually become a game-changing channel for us. Instead of quitting in month nine, I'd rather keep going because every attempt makes me better.
- **Hiring:** Hiring Saana as my operations manager was a gamble— one that didn't just double efficiency, but multiplied our capacity across the entire business. Because the right person doesn't add; they compound.
- **PR and visibility:** PR is always a bet—you can't predict the impact, outcome, or results. You put in the work, pitch the right angles, build relationships, and trust that the long-term visibility builds momentum over time.

Some of these bets hit right away. Others took longer. A few didn't work out at all. But every single one taught me something valuable and helped me refine my strategy.

Now, just because I say scaling is about making bets, that doesn't mean you should take risks blindly. You need to create structure so your risks have a foundation to land on. I mapped out my business like a well-oiled machine—documenting processes, clarifying roles, and streamlining operations.

The combination of strategic bets layered on top of solid systems is what creates sustainable growth. It's what turns scaling from a gamble into a strategy.

Building a Unique Ability Team

One of the most powerful breakthroughs in scaling a business is learning to build a *Unique Ability Team*—a concept popularized by Dan Sullivan. The core idea is simple: Every team member should operate in their zone of genius, focusing on the work that feels like play to them. When people are doing work they love and are naturally gifted at, their performance skyrockets—and so does the company's growth.

Most small businesses start with team members wearing multiple hats. Someone might do "a little bit of sales, a little bit of marketing, and a little bit of client work." This might get you through the early stages, but it won't take you to scale. As your company grows, this lack of clarity doesn't bode well.

To scale sustainably, each role must have a single, clear focus. Your client success managers should be entirely focused on client results. Your sales team should be fully dedicated to closing deals. Your marketing team should concentrate solely on generating leads and building brand awareness. When everyone knows exactly what success looks like in their role—and they have measurable KPIs to track progress—you create clarity across the entire organization. That clarity gives you the confidence to sell more, knowing that every new client will have a consistent, high-quality experience.

But it's not just about finding people who *can* do the job. It's about hiring people who *love* the job.

For example, when filling our executive assistant role, we didn't just look for someone who was "organized" or "good with people." We hired someone who genuinely *loves* spreadsheets, someone who gets excited about the details that most people find tedious. Because for them, what looks like work to others feels like play. That passion translates into excellence, and that excellence compounds as your company grows.

Over time, my hiring philosophy shifted. I no longer look for employees who simply "get the job done." I seek out people whose ambition matches with my vision and who bring their unique ability to the table. When every team member is deeply engaged in their role, it's a win-win all around.

The difference this makes is remarkable. Recently, we had a monthly team meeting where the energy in the room was electric. Everyone was excited, focused, and engaged. That same week, we had our *highest sales week in two years*. The numbers were impressive, but what really struck me was the *how*: We surpassed our 2022 performance without the hustle, stress, or chaos that characterized our earlier growth years. This time, the success came from leadership and having the right people in the right roles.

Steve Jobs once explained what happens when you build a company with extraordinary people: "I found that when you get enough A-players together…they really like working with each other. They don't want to work with B- and C-players, so it becomes self-policing."

Your first ten people set the tone for everything that follows. When those first hires are true A-players—deeply talented, intrinsically motivated, and energized by one another—you create the foundation for something remarkable, whether your vision is a $10 million company or a self-led business that generates $1–2 million per year.

The principle remains the same: Don't cut corners on people.

Heini's Story: From Survival Mode to Sustainable Scale

When Heini joined my program in the fall of 2024, she wasn't a beginner. She had seven years of experience running a brick-and-mortar fitness and wellness business. From the outside, it looked like success: her own gym, loyal members, and full days. Inside, however, the numbers told a different story. Her business was exhausting and structurally impossible to scale without breaking her.

Before moving into a new location, she ran the numbers and realized something devastating: They would lose $10,000 every single month. Her model—$47 gym memberships, $250 personal training packages, and a "premium" offer of more personal training sessions for $499— could never sustain the overhead or the hours. Even that $499 offer felt so expensive to her at the time that when someone finally bought it, she remembers thinking, *Who would ever pay this much?*

The business consumed her evenings and weekends. She could never step away, never breathe, never imagine a future that wasn't tied to the gym's walls. Eventually, the pressure caught up with her. Burnout hit hard, followed by the stress of navigating a near-bankruptcy. It was the kind of turning point that forces brutal honesty: *This cannot be my life.*

After closing that door, Heini knew exactly what she didn't want: no more tiny-ticket offers, no more trading time for money, no more paying for walls and equipment that ate up every dollar the business brought in, and no more building a company that only worked if she was physically present. She'd already been exposed to the idea of premium coaching programs, and the question wouldn't leave her alone: *Could I really earn thousands from a single client?* That curiosity became her entry point into Smart Mentoring.

The shift happened quickly, but it wasn't random. Her first pilot launch during our twelve-week program brought in $28,000—more than she had ever earned in such a short period of time. It wasn't just money that changed things. It was the realization that her new business model didn't require more hours or more exhaustion. It was scalable by design.

Her early breakthroughs centered around the same foundations this book highlights: deeply understanding her ideal client, packaging her expertise into a high-value transformation, using social media intentionally instead of reactively, and running structured, meaningful sales conversations that uncovered what clients truly wanted. None of it was flashy. All of it was systemized. And because of that, it worked.

One of her biggest bets came around pricing. When she and her business partner created a new program, they planned to price it around

$3,000–$3,500. In coaching, we challenged her to try $5,000 instead. At first, she resisted. It felt unrealistic and almost embarrassing to say out loud. But she tried it anyway. Within a few weeks, they sold sixteen out of seventeen spots at the higher price, generating nearly $80,000. That moment cracked open an old belief she had been carrying for years: "Anyone could do what I do." For the first time, she saw her expertise was valuable, rare, and in demand.

As her revenue grew, Heini began building a team. She learned one of the hardest lessons for any founder: Freedom doesn't come from hiring people to "help"; it comes from delegating ownership so she can stay in her zone of genius. She passed on administrative tasks, invoicing, sales calls, and even delivery responsibilities, keeping only the work she loved most—leadership and high-impact coaching. By May 2025, her systems were so dialed in that she joked she felt almost "unemployed." The business ran without her needing to hold every piece together.

Now, not everything was smooth. After working with a business partner under a shared brand, she realized their values didn't match and made the difficult but necessary decision to walk away. She took delivery back into her own hands temporarily, and within a week, clients were sending glowing feedback.

Today, Heini runs a business that once felt impossible to her. A million-dollar year no longer feels like a fantasy; it feels like a strategic decision she could make at any moment. She works from home or from her second base in Lapland. Coaching calls happen on walking trails. She's planning retreats in Tenerife. She chooses her clients, builds her schedule around her energy, and leads a company designed around the life she wants to live, not the other way around.

Financially, she went from $2,000 in the bank to more than $60,000 in reserves, all while paying herself and her team consistently. But the real transformation is who she's become. She no longer runs toward burnout to feel productive. She no longer doubts the value of her work. She no longer believes she needs to do everything alone. More importantly, she's no longer just "running a business." She's building a scalable business that can grow with or without her—a business designed for the long game.

When women ask her how she created this level of freedom, her answer is simple: "Let go of control. Trust other people. And get a mentor early so you don't spend years smashing your head against the wall."

Extend Your Timeframe

When you play the infinite game mentioned earlier, it changes your relationship with time. Instead of asking, "How fast can I grow?" you start asking, "What needs to be true for this business to still work, at a higher level, five or ten years from now?" That question naturally leads you away from shortcuts and toward systems that can actually support long-term growth.

Many entrepreneurs struggle with scaling not because their vision is too big, but because their timeline is too short. When you try to force sustainable growth into a two-year window, you create urgency that leads to rushed hiring, weak systems, and decisions that don't hold up under pressure.

Remember to play the infinite game. Extending the timeframe changes the decisions you make. You stop chasing short-term wins and start focusing on what compounds: process, team, delivery, infrastructure. These aren't the most exciting moves in the moment, but they are the ones that make real scaling possible.

This shift also changes how you measure progress. You stop judging success by a single launch or a single week and start looking at patterns over months and years. That perspective makes it easier to stay consistent, to refine what isn't working, and to let strong systems do their job.

How I Played the Infinite Game

The year 2025 was our fastest growth yet. By May, we had already crossed half a million dollars in revenue, and in one record-breaking week, we brought in $58,000—with $30,000 of that collected in cash. That number shattered our previous record of $50,000, which we set back in 2022.

But back in 2022, those results felt like a fluke. I couldn't fully explain why we'd hit those numbers or how to repeat them. It was like throwing darts in the dark and sometimes, by luck, hitting the target.

Now, things are different. When we have a strong week today, I know *exactly* why. I can trace every piece of it back to specific actions, campaigns, and systems. That clarity is priceless because it means the results aren't random anymore—they're *repeatable*. Honestly, I'd rather fail and understand why than succeed without a clue how to do it again.

A huge part of that shift came from extending my timeframe and playing the infinite game. For years, I was fixated on the numbers day-to-day, constantly asking, *Where are the leads this week? Why aren't sales higher today?* That short-term, finite mindset kept me in a constant state of stress and reaction.

What I've learned is that results don't appear overnight. What you see today is the product of what you did 90 to 180 days ago. That means when you make a big move—like raising prices, launching a new offer, or hiring a key team member—you won't see the payoff immediately. You have to commit and give it time to work.

For example, when we brought in consultants to overhaul our client delivery systems, they warned me upfront: "It will take two to three full rounds before you see a real shift." In our twelve-week program, that meant six months before we'd feel the full impact. If I hadn't embraced that timeline, I might have abandoned the changes halfway through, convinced they weren't working, when in reality they just needed more time to take root.

These days, I no longer judge success by what happens in a single week. If a webinar flops or a campaign underperforms, I don't panic or blame my team. Instead, I look at the system. A failed launch is a signal that the process needs refinement. My role as the leader is to trust the team, keep improving the system, and let the results compound over time.

Becoming the Person Who Can Scale

While scaling is about systems, strategy, or hiring the right team, it's also about *you*. It requires you to grow into the person who can confidently hold a bigger vision and lead at a higher level.

One of the most surprising things I've experienced is how quickly the extraordinary becomes normal. When we hit our highest sales week ever, I expected to feel wildly different. Instead, it felt…routine. What once seemed like a huge, impossible milestone simply became part of the rhythm of the business.

That's the mindset shift that scaling demands: asking yourself, *Who is the person who can do this with ease? Who is the leader who doesn't need to push or hustle frantically, but can guide the business calmly and intentionally?*

It's very much like the leap you made when you first went from employee to entrepreneur. Back then, you had to take a bold risk, stepping into the unknown with no guarantees. Scaling is the next version of that leap. You can't half-commit or just "see how it goes." You need to be all in, willing to take risks, make tough calls, and step into discomfort once again.

The challenge is that success brings comfort. When you've built something stable, it's tempting to protect what you have instead of reaching for more. But growth requires you to leave that comfort zone behind.

Growing a Business Is an Art Project

If you're in the thick of building your business right now, it can feel like a constant uphill climb—sleepless nights, pressure to perform, and the nagging question of whether you're getting it "right." I've been there, and I know how heavy that can feel.

But it doesn't have to stay that way.

One shift completely changed how I view entrepreneurship. I started seeing my business as a giant art project. When you approach it this way, it becomes less about perfection and more about creativity, exploration, and growth. Think about how you feel when you're deeply engaged in something creative—you're pulled in because you *want* to give it your all, not because you're weighed down by fear or stress.

Of course, challenges still come up, and yes, there are still stressful moments. But my relationship to that stress is different now. Even in tough seasons, my husband has noticed the change. In earlier years, I would spiral into panic when things got hard. Now, I'm able to move through challenges one day at a time, trusting the process and believing things will improve, mostly because I've seen myself overcome obstacles before.

If you're feeling overwhelmed, I want you to take this to heart: The pressure you feel today isn't permanent. Over time, you'll build resilience and confidence. When you treat your business like an art project, you give yourself permission to experiment, to play, and to create something extraordinary.

Key Takeaways

#1. Scaling magnifies your weak spots.

Growth doesn't create problems, it amplifies them. If your systems are shaky or your processes unclear, scaling will make those cracks even bigger. Strengthen your foundation first by addressing issues one at a time. When you focus on fixing problems early, growth becomes smoother and more sustainable, allowing you to scale with confidence rather than chaos.

#2. Build a team around unique abilities.

Scaling happens when everyone operates in their zone of genius. Create a team where each person focuses on what they do best, rather than trying to do everything. This creates a business that runs smoothly and delivers consistent results. When your team's strengths are supported by clear systems and a shared vision, scaling becomes sustainable and far less stressful.

#3. Extend your timeline.

Big goals take time. When you try to hit massive targets too quickly, you make rushed decisions and create unnecessary stress. By extending your timeline, you remove pressure and allow space for strategic, thoughtful moves. Ironically, giving yourself more time often helps you reach your goals faster because you build a stronger foundation and make smarter, long-term choices.

#4. Scaling is about making bets.
Every decision you make in scaling—hiring, launching a new offer, or raising prices—is a bet on your future. Some bets will pay off; others won't. The key is to stay agile, learn quickly, and adjust as you go.

#5. Become the person your future business needs.
Scaling requires personal growth just as much as business growth. The strategies that got you to one level won't get you to the next. You must step into a bigger role—leading with confidence, taking risks, and holding the vision for what's ahead. The more you grow personally, the more capable you become of guiding your business into the future.

Strategies & Tools
When it comes to scaling, your systems are the foundation. With them, growth becomes sustainable. Without them, growth will only amplify your problems.

One way to think about this is to start with the organizational chart. For example, to run a $1 million per year business, you don't need a massive team. You could get there with a handful of key roles:

- 1–2 Sales Closers
- 1–2 Appointment Setters
- 1–2 Client Success/Access Managers
- 1 Executive Assistant
- Optional: 1 Marketing Assistant (depending on your business model)

With this lean team, I was able to run my company for several years without an operations manager. That role only became necessary once the team grew larger and more complex.

Beyond the people, you also need systems for the business itself. The next three tools—the Issues List, the Smart Scale 90-Day Operating Review, and a practical method for defining KPIs in non-revenue roles—will help you build that structure.

Issues List

An issues list is one of the simplest tools for running and scaling a business. It's a living document where you capture every problem, bottleneck, or friction point across the company so you can address issues proactively rather than reacting when something breaks. Instead of carrying everything in your head, you create a single place where problems are visible, ranked, and turned into real decisions. This list becomes your roadmap for what to fix before you scale, ensuring you're not amplifying dysfunction at a larger size.

To create your issues list, set up a simple spreadsheet and use the following columns to evaluate and prioritize each item:

- **Problem:** What isn't working?
- **Current state:** What does this look like right now?
- **Impact if unsolved:** What happens if you ignore it?
- **Suggested solution (project):** Your proposed path forward.
- **The best outcome:** What success would look like.
- **Benefit/Value:** Why it matters for revenue, operations, or morale.
- **Cost/Effort:** Roughly how much time, money, or energy the fix requires.
- **Timeline:** How long the fix will take.
- **Importance ranking:** Helps identify what should move first.
- **Notes:** Any additional context or updates.

Once the list exists, the key is to actually use it. Add issues as they emerge, update the list at least once a month, and use it to decide what becomes a priority for each quarter. Every ninety days, identify the top recurring problems and turn them into your focus areas.

Even small issues—confusing handoffs, messy reporting, inefficient tools—belong here, because these are the things that drain energy and prevent the team from operating at its best. Over time, working from an issues list builds a far more proactive, self-correcting company. When you know what's slowing you down, you know what to fix. And when you know what to fix, scaling becomes far smoother and far more intentional.

Smart Scale 90-Day Operating Review

The Smart Scale 90-Day Operating Review is a simple quarterly ritual that helps you step out of the day-to-day and assess your business with clarity. Instead of sprinting from task to task, this review gives you space to evaluate what's working, what isn't, and what needs your focus next. It's designed to keep you connected to your long-term vision while ensuring you're making meaningful progress every quarter.

The review follows seven steps:

1. Reality check

Start by getting honest about where you are right now. Look at the facts, which include your revenue, profit, fulfillment capacity, team size, energy levels, and overall workload. Identify what's draining you and what still depends entirely on you. The goal is simple: Gain radical clarity on your current operating reality so you know exactly what you're working with.

2. Celebrate and extract lessons

Before you decide what to change, identify what went well. Review your wins from the last ninety days, and pinpoint the choices, systems, or habits that led to progress. Then look at what didn't go as planned (this is where you fill the issues list) and extract the lesson. If you had to relive the last quarter, what would you repeat and what would you do differently? This step helps you turn experience into structured learning.

3. Focus and intent

Choose your direction for the next ninety days. Identify the *one* strategic goal that, if accomplished, makes everything else easier or unnecessary.

From there, define two to three key results that will signal success. Determine what systems, people, or skills you need to support that goal, and decide how you'll measure weekly momentum. The goal here is to create a clear focus and measurable next steps.

4. Vision clarity (twelve months out)

Zoom out and imagine where you want your business to be one year from now if you execute consistently. Consider revenue, team structure, offers, and your day-to-day lifestyle. Do the same for your personal life; what role do you want to be operating in a year from now? Identify the decisions you need to make *now* to support that future version. Capture "winning the year" in one sentence. The goal here is to connect quarterly actions to annual vision.

5. The long game (three-year view)

Extend your horizon to three years. What kind of business are you truly building—team-driven, scalable, global-impact, or lifestyle-focused? What do you want your life to look like? Identify what you want to stop doing entirely and what you want to spend most of your time on. Consider how you want your company to be described and what capabilities or partnerships need to be built today to make that vision real. This step anchors your near-term work inside your long-term North Star.

6. Integration: The founder's transformation

Scaling isn't only about mechanics; it's about identity. Clarify the personal shift required for you to operate at your next level. Who is the version of you who easily achieves these goals? What habits, fears, or control tendencies do you need to release? And what new beliefs, environments, or routines will support you in the next ninety days? Each quarter becomes an upgrade not just for your business, but for you as a founder.

7. Action sprint

Finally, turn the vision into execution. Choose three to five clear priorities for the next ninety days and assign ownership to your team (focusing on *who*, not *how*). Schedule checkpoints at thirty, sixty, and ninety days to keep momentum on track. Block out a monthly "Day After Tomorrow" session—time dedicated to working on the future of the business instead of getting lost in daily operations.

Defining KPIs for Non-Revenue Roles

One of the questions founders often ask is how to set measurable KPIs for roles that don't have direct revenue responsibility—positions like operations, executive assistance, or project coordination. These roles are essential to the company's ability to scale, yet their success is harder to quantify because the work is ongoing, supportive, and often behind the scenes. But this is exactly why clarity matters.

When a role has well-defined KPIs, two powerful things happen:

1. Ownership becomes unmistakably clear, and
2. The team member gains genuine autonomy.

It's a win–win. The founder gains visibility into what "success" looks like, and the team member knows what they are responsible for without needing constant direction. This clarity is foundational when you're building a self-led team.

Below is an example of how to create KPIs for a role with no direct revenue metrics, such as an Executive Assistant:

- Bookkeeping reports are delivered to the CEO by the fifteenth of each month, with 100 percent of accounting completed for the current fiscal period.
- No more than $30,000 in overdue invoices (over five days).
- Email response time under twenty-four hours on weekdays.
- The CEO's calendar is organized for both the current and upcoming week, with all recurring events scheduled six months in advance.
- Proactively removes at least seven tasks from the CEO's desk each month without being asked.

These KPIs are simple, practical, and measurable. But the deeper shift here is how you define ownership. True ownership means responsibility for outcomes, not individual tasks. For example, instead of "upload receipts to accounting," the KPI might be framed as "ensure all financial communication and coordination between internal and external stakeholders runs smoothly and deadlines are met."

Task ownership keeps people in a narrow lane, waiting for instructions. Outcome ownership empowers them to take initiative, identify issues before you see them, and think like leaders. This is how you build a self-led team—people who don't wait for permission, but own the entire result.

Final Thoughts

Scaling is about building a business that gets stronger as it grows. When your systems, team, and vision are working together, scaling stops feeling like a scramble and starts feeling sustainable. The breakthroughs you experience aren't just about hitting bigger numbers either; they're about creating a business that can operate without you constantly holding it together.

This chapter has been about the long game: fixing cracks before they widen, placing smart bets, and learning to think in years instead of weeks. Scaling done right gives you something far more valuable than a record sales week—it gives you freedom. The freedom to lead instead of hustle. The freedom to grow without breaking. The freedom to take a step back, knowing your business will continue to thrive.

But sustainable growth isn't just about the business side. As your company expands, so do the demands on your time, energy, and relationships. The next breakthrough isn't just professional—it's personal. In the next chapter, we'll explore how to structure your business so that growth supports your life instead of competing with it, ensuring your success doesn't come at the expense of your health, happiness, or the life you're working so hard to build.

CHAPTER 10

DESIGNING A LIFE YOU DON'T NEED TO ESCAPE FROM

At the start of 2025, I decided to try an experiment I'd heard a business influencer who promotes hustle culture rave about: Work one hundred days straight. No weekends, no breaks, just relentless hustle. The idea was that pushing nonstop would create unstoppable momentum.

So I thought, *Why not? Let's see if this really works.*

Spoiler alert: It didn't.

I didn't even make it halfway. By day forty-five, I was cooked. My brain wasn't sparking with new ideas—it was barely limping along. Sundays were swallowed by sales calls. My calendar was jammed with tasks my team could have handled without me. And somehow, I convinced myself this was "scaling."

What was I thinking?

Instead of momentum, I got exhaustion. Instead of breakthroughs, I ran out of clarity. This experiment easily revealed how working every day wasn't growing my company. In fact, it was suffocating it.

So, I quit the challenge. I took back my weekends. And you know what happened? My energy returned. My creativity returned. The business started to grow again—not because I was doing *more*, but because I was finally doing *less of the wrong things*.

In this chapter, we'll challenge the traditional idea of work-life balance and reframe it through the lens of entrepreneurship. That balance isn't static or symmetrical; it's seasonal, intentional, and alive. You'll learn how to define success on your own terms, create a rhythm that matches your season of life, and build a business that grows without demanding every ounce of your time and energy.

Defining Success and Building Around That

As entrepreneurs, one of the greatest privileges we have is the ability to define what success looks like and then design our lives and businesses around that vision.

For me, this journey has always been about building a life on my terms. From the moment I found out I was pregnant with my first child, I started thinking ahead. What would my days look like as a mom and a business owner? I didn't want to miss kindergarten events or feel chained to my laptop while my family lived life without me. I wanted to be present, to have flexibility, and to make decisions based on my values, not my calendar.

The clearer you are about what success means to you, the easier it is to reverse engineer it. For me, success doesn't mean endless grinding. It means building a modern business that supports the lifestyle I want—a way of working that feels connected to who I am and how I want to live.

Over the years, people have told me I'm doing things "the modern entrepreneur way." Even some older clients have hired me because they wanted to be surrounded by that mindset. And honestly, that feels good, because it proves there isn't just one path to building something meaningful.

I've heard plenty of limiting beliefs along the way, especially from men in mastermind groups. Some will say things like, "I don't even want to marry my girlfriend or have kids because they'll distract me from my business." I always smile at that because my life is living proof that it doesn't have to be true. I have two kids, a marriage, and a business that continues to grow year after year.

To me, those relationships don't hold me back—they actually sharpen my focus. When you have other priorities, you don't have time to waste. You cut the fluff. You focus on what truly matters. Having kids has forced me to be more focused with my energy, and my business has grown because of it.

Early on, plenty of people told me, "You can't do that." And time after time, I've proven them wrong. So when I hear the relentless "grind" message pushed online—the idea that you have to sacrifice everything and work 24/7—I stop and ask, "Is that really true?" Maybe it's easier to grow quickly without kids or outside commitments, but that doesn't make it the only way.

We need more diverse role models showing different versions of success. The younger generation deserves to see that you don't have to hustle yourself into burnout to build a thriving business. You can build something that supports the life you actually want to live and the freedom that it affords you.

But freedom isn't about doing less work; it's about having choice. Today, I don't *have* to work late nights or weekends, but sometimes I choose to because I'm excited about what I'm building. The difference is that it's on my terms.

The Entrepreneur's Work-Life Balance

Work-life balance looks very different for entrepreneurs than it does for people who work a traditional job. When you're an employee, your days are often structured for you. You know when you clock in, when you clock out, and what's expected in between. Balance, in that world, can sometimes mean simply leaving work at work and being fully present at home.

But when you're an entrepreneur, the lines are blurrier and more flexible. We don't have balance. We have rhythms. Some days, the business demands everything from you. You might work late into the night or spend an entire weekend focused on a launch. Other days, life takes the lead. When your kids are home sick, when summer break rolls around, or when there's a family milestone you don't want to miss, you shift gears and build your schedule around those priorities.

For example, when my older daughter was home from kindergarten for nearly two months over summer, I mapped out my weeks to make space for that. I knew the few essential outcomes I needed to deliver—like hosting a weekly webinar—and I delegated everything else to my team. With this planning, I was able to spend my days playing with my kids and soaking up that precious summertime with them.

The truth is, if you try to keep a perfectly even balance every single day, you'll probably never build anything meaningful. Entrepreneurship happens in seasons (more on this soon). There will be periods when the business needs you to sprint, like when you pour in long hours and stretch yourself to meet big goals. And then there will be periods when you can slow down, rest, and give more of your energy to family, health, and personal growth.

Balance, for me, isn't measured in twenty-four-hour increments. It shows up over the long term. Looking back over a year, I want to see that I've poured deeply into both my business and my family, even if some individual days or weeks felt lopsided.

I've also come to accept that choosing this path may have slowed my growth compared to others. Could I have scaled faster if I'd never taken maternity leave or paused to focus on my family? Probably. But those pauses were worth it. The business might have grown at a slower pace, but it has grown on *my terms*.

And I couldn't do it alone. I'm fortunate to have a husband who shares the load, from school drop-offs to birthday party planning. I know this would be far more challenging without that support, and I deeply respect single parents who juggle both roles.

Ultimately, work-life balance as an entrepreneur is about sustainability. It's about building a life and a business that you can grow with for years to come. Some seasons you'll sprint, and others you'll rest.

Your Freedom Isn't Selfish

One of the biggest mindset shifts you'll make as an entrepreneur is realizing that your freedom isn't a luxury or something you have to "earn." It's part of your responsibility.

Your role is fundamentally different from your team's. You're the one who took the risk, built the infrastructure, created the jobs, and ultimately carries responsibility for every difficult situation. Even when you're not technically working, the business is still on your mind: every challenge, every opportunity, every next step. That kind of weight requires stamina, perspective, and long-term endurance.

If you try to live by exactly the same rules as your team members, you'll burn yourself out. Team members can clock out, rest, reset, and even leave if things get too stressful. You don't have that option. The responsibility stays with you, which means you have to be intentional about protecting your energy. Taking a long lunch, taking a weekend off, or keeping your mornings open isn't selfish. It's how you ensure the company stays healthy. Freedom isn't therefore a reward; it's a necessity so you can carry the responsibility no one else carries.

Your job isn't to be "equal" either. Your job is to stay strong enough to hold the vision, make the hard decisions, and keep the business moving forward.

I used to feel pressure to be "equal" with my team and match their hours, like being in the office from 8 a.m. to 4 p.m. when I could have taken a day off. But when a team member leaves, the work and the unresolved issues stay with me. When I step away, nothing actually leaves. I still carry the responsibility, the decisions, the direction. Realizing this helped me drop the guilt. My freedom isn't indulgence. My freedom is what allows me to show up with energy and clarity for everyone else.

Here are some action steps you can take to reinforce this in your own business:

- Write down what your ideal daily rhythm looks like, and map out the steps to make it real.
- Make a clear internal distinction: Your responsibilities and your rules will never look the same as your team's.
- Communicate openly with your team: The entrepreneur's role is different, so the structure around that role has to be different.
- If someone struggles with this, be direct: Entrepreneur freedom and employee freedom can't be compared, because the responsibilities are not the same.

Freedom isn't a reward. It's how you stay in the game long enough to lead well.

Tips for Finding Your Rhythm as an Entrepreneur

You find your own rhythm by creating systems, building trust, and empowering others so you don't have to carry it all alone. Over the years, I've discovered a few key practices that have made the biggest difference in maintaining a healthy flow between my business and my personal life.

1. Protect your time off.

When you take time off, *truly* take time off. No Slack. No emails. No "just checking in." Last year, I went completely offline for two full weeks while on a family trip to Thailand. While my aim was to rest and enjoy the vacation, it was also a bit of a test. I wanted to see if the company could run without me. Could my team handle decisions? Would the systems we'd built actually hold up? These breaks reveal where your business still depends on you too much. If something falls apart while you're away, look at that as feedback on what needs to be fixed or corrected.

2. Build a self-sustaining business.

You should always build your business as if you were going to sell it someday, even if you never plan to. That mindset forces you to build processes, documentation, and systems that make the business valuable and functional without your constant presence. When you can step away and things keep running smoothly, you know you've built something scalable.

3. Stop treating everything like an emergency.

One of my mentors once told me, "Nothing is an emergency in this business." That helped me shift out of panic mode and allowed me to make calmer, more strategic decisions. Very few things in an expert-based business are truly urgent. When you let go of the constant rush, you free yourself from unnecessary stress while giving your team breathing room too.

4. Delegate at home just like you do at work.
Finding a rhythm doesn't only happen inside the business. It starts at home. I'm not the mom who obsesses over perfectly braided hair or Pinterest-worthy outfits. My priority is that my kids are happy, content, and fed. Sometimes that means letting my husband dress them in outfits that make me laugh. We've divided responsibilities clearly: He checks the kindergarten app, manages school notifications, and only sends me calendar invites if there's something I absolutely need to know.

5. Trust others to rise to the occasion.
Whether it's your operations manager or your spouse, delegation helps you free yourself from tasks, and it also empowers others. When people feel trusted, they step up. The same way my team takes ownership of the business, my husband takes ownership of things at home. When you let go of control, you create space for others to shine.

Working in Seasons

One of the most powerful shifts I've made as an entrepreneur is learning to see my life and business in *seasons* rather than expecting perfect rhythm every single day. For a long time, I believed weekends automatically counted as free time. But I'd find myself sneaking in just one quick task—answering an email, tweaking a project plan—and suddenly, that day wasn't free at all.

Now, I plan my time with much more intention. Some weeks, I might only get one true free day, while other weeks—like during midsummer celebrations—I'll take three in a row. The point isn't to have the same schedule every week. The point is to recognize and honor the season I'm in. Giving myself permission to *lean in* when the business needs me and *pull back* when family or rest takes priority, I've realized that finding a flow or rhythm isn't about doing the exact same thing every day. In fact, trying to force a rigid idea of "balance" often created more stress for me. It's far less stressful to fully commit to the work season when it's here and then fully unplug during slower seasons.

If I look back at my calendar in 2024, it almost feels like a different life. Back then, my days had a slower rhythm. I worked just four to six hours a day, usually in the mornings until about noon—or maybe two o'clock at the latest. After that, my afternoons were completely free. I had long weekends, too.

For midsummer, I took nearly a full week off—from Wednesday through Monday—completely unplugged. It was a season filled with space. Space to be with my family, to rest, to recharge. And yet, the business kept moving forward. It was proof that growth doesn't always have to mean chaos.

In 2025, my calendar looked completely different. My mornings started early, with a workout at 7 a.m.—either CrossFit or Megaformer Pilates. By 8 o'clock, I was at my desk, working straight through until about 4 p.m. After school pickup, I switched gears and spent time fully present with my kids, focused on family until bedtime.

But when the house got quiet again, I dived back in. I replaced TV time with writing this book, preparing materials, and tackling the projects that move my business forward. Saturdays became my one indulgence, the night I saved for my favorite shows as a small reward for the week's work.

It was a sacrifice, yes, but a deliberate one. Instead of taking time away from my kids when they're awake, I took it from the evenings. That choice allowed me to show up for my family during the day while still pursuing my bigger goals at night.

I love how Dan Sullivan explains this using an athlete and artist framework. Athletes don't compete every single day. They have focus days for peak performance, buffer days for training and preparation, and free days for recovery. Artists are similar: There are show days, rehearsal days, and days of pure rest.

When I compare these two years, I see a rhythm in both, just expressed differently. While 2024 was about slower days and long stretches of time off, 2025 was about discipline, sacrifice, and scaling.

Neither season is better or worse. The key is recognizing which season you're in and intentionally adjusting your time to match it. That's how you create a rhythm that truly works for you.

Building a Sustainable Culture for Your Team

Creating a sustainable rhythm for yourself is only one part of the equation. The other is building a company culture where your team can design their work in a way that fits their own lives, pace, and seasons.

Everyone on my team works remotely or in a flexible hybrid setup and sets their own schedule. We have a beautiful office in Helsinki, but the team is free to use it whenever it suits them. Yes, we have general hours when most of us are online, but there's room for real life. One of my team members, for example, is a single mom in Portugal, so mornings are busy with school drop-offs and routines. She doesn't make our weekly team meetings and instead watches the recordings later. That works fine because, for me, what matters is performance and results, not sitting at a desk at a certain hour.

Another team member, our operations manager, once brought her baby to an offsite so she could breastfeed between sessions. It was seamless because we've created an environment where people can integrate their work and life without guilt.

Of course, freedom comes with responsibility. I don't track anyone's hours, but I expect everyone to manage their energy and workload. If someone overworks one week, they take time off later. This works because we've built clarity into everything: clear role descriptions, expectations, and KPIs. Everyone knows what success looks like in their role, which prevents misunderstandings and endless difficult conversations.

This clarity also empowers team members to make decisions about their own capacity. When one mom realized she couldn't meet the expectations of her role with a newborn at home, she chose to step away on her own. There was no drama because the standards were transparent from the start.

I've mentioned this in previous chapters, but it's worth repeating: Hiring the right people is essential to this kind of culture. A high-performing team naturally elevates the group. They don't need micromanaging, because they care deeply about their work. If they miss something on Friday, they'll fix it on Sunday without me ever having to ask—not because they have to, but because they *want* to.

For many of my team members, this job truly is a dream. My client success manager was once a client herself. Now she spends her days doing what she loves most: coaching clients and helping them achieve results without the stress of marketing or sales. My closers get to focus entirely on sales. Everyone stays in their zone of genius while enjoying the flexibility of an entrepreneurial lifestyle—without needing to carry the weight of being *the* entrepreneur.

This is why turnover in my company is so low. People don't want to leave. My role as the leader is to keep it that way. My operations manager and I stay closely connected to our team, regularly checking in on their goals, listening to their dreams, and finding ways for them to grow alongside the business.

Blending Business and Lifestyle

For me, work and life aren't two separate worlds; they naturally blend together, and I bring that same approach into my company culture. Even with my team, I want our time together to feel meaningful and enjoyable, not just "business as usual."

For example, my operations manager and I have monthly offsite meetings that mix strategy and fun. Sometimes we'll try a yoga or workout class together; other times we'll grab lunch at a nail salon so we can catch up while doing something we'd usually save for free time. These moments give us space to connect personally while still moving the business forward.

We also create shared experiences as a team. Every quarter, we plan a team day that's part celebration, part connection. Recently, we did a boxing class followed by lunch, where we shared our wins and positive focus.

That same week happened to be my operations manager Saana's thirtieth birthday, so we surprised her with cake and gifts. She later told me it meant so much because she hadn't had time to plan anything for herself.

Over the years, we've done concerts with VIP access, "Brush and Bubbles" painting sessions with champagne, and other fun outings. These experiences are intentional investments in building a culture that feels alive and human.

I don't want my business to simply provide income for me or my team. I want it to create a lifestyle—a place where work supports a life that's rich, joyful, and connected.

Vision over Rhythm

We've talked about defining success on your own terms, about how your rhythm as an entrepreneur will never look like someone else's, and about creating systems, teamwork, and seasons that support you along the way. All of those things are valuable. They give you tools to navigate the natural ebb and flow of business and life.

But at the end of the day, none of it truly matters without a clear vision.

Your vision is your North Star—the thing that guides every decision you make. It's what helps you know when to lean in, when to rest, and where to focus your energy. Without it, you end up reacting to whatever's loudest or most urgent. With it, you move intentionally, building a life and business that actually feel right for you.

From the very beginning, my motivation wasn't just about freedom or flexibility. Yes, those things are wonderful. I love that I don't need an alarm clock, that I can attend my kids' school events or take a midday CrossFit class. But those are side effects, not the point.

What truly drives me is the vision of building something that matters. Even before I had children, I wanted to create a company that could touch thousands of lives, grow into something bigger than me, and show other ambitious women what's possible. That vision continues to shape how I approach my time, my team, and my priorities.

Key Takeaways

#1. **Define success on your own terms.**
Your version of success may not look like anyone else's—and that's the point. Get clear on what you don't want and what matters most to you, and then build your business around that vision instead of letting outside voices dictate how it should look.

#2. **Rhythms are seasonal.**
Some seasons require more focus on business, others more on family or rest. Finding a sustainable rhythm that works comes from zooming out and seeing how everything fits over time, not from perfectly dividing each day.

#3. **Systems and teamwork create freedom.**
Whether at home or at work, freedom comes from delegation and trust. Build systems so that both your business and household can run smoothly without you carrying every responsibility alone.

#4. **Your freedom is not selfish.**
Your role carries a different weight than your team's, which means your rhythm must look different too. Your freedom isn't indulgence but a part of your responsibility as a founder. Protecting your energy is what allows you to carry the long-term vision and lead your business sustainably.

#5. **Vision is your North Star.**
Your vision drives every decision and helps you navigate competing priorities. Without it, you'll drift into reaction mode. With it, you can shape your work and life with intention and clarity.

Strategies & Tools
Time Blocking Calendar

Most entrepreneurs try to manage their time by managing their tasks. But tasks are infinite. Time is not. That's why the most effective way to create flow is to design your week around three main business outcomes, connecting with others, and time for fun—not an endless to-do list.

I've experimented with nearly every project management tool and task tracker over the years. I love them for my team because they keep everyone on the same page. But for me, as a visionary leader, they've never actually worked. Instead of trying to force myself into systems that don't match how my brain works, I simplified everything.

Everything—and I mean everything—goes into my Google Calendar.

If something needs to happen, it gets a time block. If it doesn't fit into your calendar, it isn't getting done. No separate to-do lists. No sticky notes. No scattered reminders. Just a calendar that reflects reality.

Here's how to implement it yourself:

1. **Start with your non-negotiables:** Before you add work, block your personal anchors: school pickups, workouts, family time, rest blocks, appointments, and so on. These protect your energy and set the foundation for the week.
2. **Add your highest-value work blocks:** These are activities only you can do: CEO time, sales or revenue-driving work, content creation, team leadership, creative or strategic tasks. Schedule these during your peak energy hours, not random gaps between meetings.
3. **Create themed days or blocks:** Instead of switching tasks constantly, give your brain a clear rhythm. Examples: Mondays are for CEO planning and team syncing. Tuesdays are for content and creation. You get the picture. Even if your week shifts, themes give structure without rigidity.
4. **Leave white space:** Great weeks aren't "full." They're intentional. Build in buffers so you're not racing from one thing to the next. This is where creativity, problem-solving, and rest live.
5. **Treat your calendar as a commitment:** If you constantly move blocks around, you're overbooking yourself. Time blocking forces you to be honest about your capacity and make better choices.

The purpose of this system isn't to control your life but to liberate your mental bandwidth. You plan your week in advance, then simply move through each day and execute. When your calendar holds the decisions for you, you stop carrying everything in your head. You show up calmer, clearer, and far more in control of your time.

Home OS: A Household Manual

One of the biggest contributors to work-life rhythm is reducing the mental load at home. Most entrepreneurs are carrying two companies: the one they run publicly and the one they run privately. And the private one often creates the most invisible stress.

That's why my husband and I created a Household Manual, like a simple "Home Operating System" that keeps our life running smoothly without constant oversight. Think of it as documenting your home the same way you would document a business process. When everything is written down once, anyone can follow it.

Our Household Manual includes things like:

- Our favorite weekly recipes
- How we do laundry and organize clothes
- The system for washing bedding and towels
- A running grocery list of essentials
- How we prep for travel or busy weeks
- Small but important preferences, like how we like the pantry arranged or the kids' clothes sorted

This framework is especially helpful if you have a housekeeper, nanny, babysitter, or rotating support. Clear instructions mean you're not constantly managing, correcting, or reminding. You don't have to hold the entire household in your head, because your systems do.

It's essentially the same principle I use in business: Document once, delegate forever. Your home runs smoother, you save time, and your brain gets the space it needs to focus on what matters without carrying the weight of a hundred invisible tasks.

Intentional "Brain Time"

After my one-hundred-days experiment, I came out with something I have implemented ever since called "Brain Time." It represents a completely different way of thinking about productivity and well-being as an entrepreneur.

Most entrepreneurs fill their calendars with endless "doing"—calls, content, meetings, execution—and think that being busy equals being productive. But breakthroughs don't come from constant output. Breakthroughs come in moments of silence.

I learned this the hard way when I tried to work one hundred days straight. By week three, I wasn't productive at all. I was numb. My decisions got slower, my ideas got worse, and my motivation dropped. That's when I started protecting Brain Time as a non-negotiable part of my schedule.

This isn't rest in the traditional sense. It's intentional mental spaciousness—time with no inputs, no noise, and no stimulation. Time where ideas can actually land.

Brain Time can look like:

- **A walk or run without headphones.** No podcasts, no music—just space for your thoughts to settle.
- **An hour lying on the sofa just thinking.** Not meditating, not scrolling—simply giving your mind room to wander.
- **Completely free days with zero work-related thinking.** True mental detachment.

What I've also realized is that the bigger the goal, the more Brain Time you need. When you're leading a growing company or aiming for 10x outcomes, your main job isn't to do but to think better. And better thinking requires space. That's why Brain Time isn't just about self-care. It's a performance strategy—one that allows entrepreneurs to stay clear, creative, and focused enough to actually reach those big goals without burning out.

And the best part is that anyone can implement it. Start with one hour a week. Then two. Then a half day. Train your brain to operate with more spaciousness and less noise. Your creativity will return. Your thinking will strengthen. And your decisions will improve dramatically.

Final Thoughts

My failed one-hundred-days experiment showed me that a work-life rhythm isn't about cramming more hours into the day or proving how hard you can push. Instead, you should be aiming for clarity: knowing what matters most and making intentional choices about where your energy goes. Some seasons will require sprinting, while others will allow for rest and slower, more spacious days.

We've explored what it looks like to build rhythm, sustainability, and flow into your own life and extend that same freedom to your team. Along the way, we've talked about seasons, vision, and the power of defining success on your own terms.

But nothing really matters unless you have a rock-solid vision. When you lead with vision and design both your business and your lifestyle around it, you stop chasing someone else's expectations and give yourself permission to have fun again. Looking back, I can see that quitting that one-hundred-days challenge was a decision to stop buying into someone else's definition of success and instead create my own.

And that, more than any hustle or hack, was just another breakthrough of my entrepreneurial journey.

CONCLUSION

When we first begin our entrepreneurial journeys, we often imagine breakthroughs as dramatic turning points—these cinematic moments where everything suddenly falls into place. But in reality, breakthroughs look and feel much quieter than that. They show up as subtle shifts inside you long before the numbers catch up. They're the moments when you stop asking, "How do I do everything?" and start asking, "What does my business need from me next?" They're the times you notice yourself letting go of old habits—not because someone told you to, but because you finally feel ready to move differently.

In the early days, your effort mattered more than anything. You were the entire engine of the business—showing up with grit and determination even when you didn't fully believe in yourself yet. You did every role because you had to. There's nothing wrong with that season. It builds instincts and resilience you'll rely on for years.

But that season isn't meant to last forever.

Eventually, the very skills that helped you survive start keeping you small. Many brilliant experts reach this moment and feel the tension—you know you need a different way forward, but you're afraid to let go of the familiar patterns: the constant doing, the juggling, the feeling that everything depends on your effort. When exhaustion creeps in, it's not a sign you're failing. It's a sign you've outgrown the way you built your business.

My hope is that this book has been a gentle guide—helping you see your next steps with more clarity and less fear. Every strategy, every framework, every story has been pointing you somewhere deeper: toward a business you can trust and toward a version of yourself who leads with calm, clarity, and confidence instead of urgency.

Because real breakthroughs don't come from pushing harder. They come from knowing where you're heading and making decisions that support that direction. They come from intention instead of impulse. They come from allowing yourself to slow down long enough to build something that lasts.

Looking back, you may realize that the decisions you once treated as small—raising your prices, documenting a process, saying no to the wrong client, hiring someone before you felt ready—were actually tiny hinges that opened big doors. They didn't feel dramatic, but they were pivotal. Those quiet choices are the ones that shape sustainable success.

And as you continue, I want you to anchor into this truth: You didn't get here by accident. You've already proven that you can take action without perfect clarity. You've already shown that you're willing to grow even when it's uncomfortable. You've built the capacity to lead at a higher level, whether you see it fully yet or not.

Growth will still challenge you. There will be moments when doubt creeps in or old patterns try to pull you back. But now you have something you didn't have before: awareness. You can see the difference between chaos and clarity, between reacting and leading, between doing everything and choosing what truly matters.

That awareness is the beginning of every future breakthrough.

Your next level won't come from squeezing more out of yourself. It will come from giving yourself space to think. From simplifying before you scale. From trusting the foundations, systems, and people you've put in place. You are not meant to sprint through your entire entrepreneurial life. You are meant to grow in seasons—seasons of building, seasons of visibility, seasons of refinement, seasons of expansion.

And as you honor each season with intention rather than urgency, you'll notice that sustainable success feels different than early success. It's quieter. More grounded. More strategic. More spacious. You stop chasing every idea. You start choosing the right ones. You stop proving yourself. You start trusting yourself. You stop holding your business together with effort and start letting it stand on the strength of what you've built.

And that is the ultimate breakthrough.

What We Learned

You began this journey with a dream: a business that didn't just survive but truly worked. One that was predictable, sustainable, and not built on the weight of doing it all yourself. Maybe that dream felt distant before, but now I hope it feels closer.

Because it is! Getting there doesn't happen by accident; it happens on purpose.

You learned that real, lasting growth comes from foundations, systems, and clarity—not hustle. You learned that the quiet decisions add up. And you learned that sustainable success is less about doing more and more about choosing wisely.

Here's a recap of what we covered:

1. **Believe Before You See It.** You anchored to your vision even without proof, and you learned that self-doubt is often a sign of growth.
2. **The First Big Breakthrough.** You saw that breakthroughs come from clarity—one offer, a clear message, simple tests, and refinement.
3. **Product and Client Fulfillment.** You built a client journey that delivers results at scale and strengthens your reputation.
4. **The Solopreneur Trap and Delegation.** You identified where you were the bottleneck and created structure so others can support you.
5. **Leadership: From Doer to Leader.** You shifted from controlling everything to providing clarity and standards.
6. **Marketing: Audience and Leads.** You focused on steady value and real conversations that attract ready buyers.
7. **Sales: Confidence and Systems.** You built a repeatable sales process grounded in your own experience.
8. **Personal Branding and PR.** You stepped into your authority through results and consistent messaging.
9. **Sustainable Success.** You strengthened your foundation with systems, people, and data.

10. **Designing a Life You Don't Need to Escape From.** You defined success on your terms and built a business that supports your life through seasons.

Your Next Breakthrough

Your journey isn't ending here. In many ways, it's just beginning. As you move forward, keep this truth close: Your next breakthrough isn't something you wait for. It's something you create—one decision, one system, one courageous step at a time.

Your next breakthrough might not even feel dramatic—and that's okay. It might be as simple as saying no to the wrong client, documenting a process for the first time, or finally raising your prices to match the value you deliver.

These decisions seem small in the moment, but they add up. They create the kind of momentum that makes growth predictable and sustainable.

Remember: The point of building a business isn't just bigger numbers. It's freedom. Freedom to work in seasons instead of nonstop hustle. Freedom to show up for your family without guilt. Freedom to take a vacation and come back to a thriving company, not a mountain of fires to put out.

That kind of freedom isn't just for other people. It's for you.

If you want support implementing these strategies, there are ways we can help.

Visit *smartmentoring.com/breakthrough*.

ACKNOWLEDGMENTS

My deepest gratitude goes to the coaches and mentors who have shaped the way I lead today—Briony McKenzie, Peter Buckle, and so many others who have expanded my thinking in ways I never could have predicted.

To my incredible team: Thank you for your creativity, your speed, your devotion to excellence, and the way you consistently raise the standard of what we deliver. You make the impossible feel simple.

A special thank you to our COO, Saana Rasehorn, for freeing my time for this project and for building the structure that allows my boldest visions to become real. With you, everything feels possible.

To every client who has trusted us with your business, your dreams, and your next level: Thank you. You are the reason we do this work. You remind us daily that what we build is bigger than the work itself, and that our impact lives through you.

To my entrepreneur friends, who understand this wild journey and walk alongside me through every season: Thank you for the candid conversations, the shared ambition, and for making the path less lonely.

To my friends outside of business and to my family: Thank you for grounding me, reminding me to laugh, and making sure I don't forget to enjoy life beyond work. You keep me human in a world that constantly asks for more.

To Avocet Books—especially Hal and Aleksandra—thank you for believing in this project and for bringing this book into fruition with such care. Your partnership, guidance, and steady support have made this book stronger in every way.

And finally, to everyone who believes in creating a life larger than their circumstances: This book exists because of people like you. To the next breakthrough.

ABOUT THE AUTHOR

Marianne Lehikoinen is a modern sales expert, entrepreneur, and the CEO and founder of Smart Mentoring, a leading sales and marketing consultancy dedicated to helping coaches, consultants, and service-based founders scale their businesses with clarity and confidence. Through her proven strategies, Marianne helps her clients transform their expertise into high-revenue, system-driven companies—without burning out, doing everything themselves, or endlessly trading time for money. Her work focuses on three core outcomes: selling high-ticket offers with integrity, building a small but mighty team, and creating consistent $20,000–$80,000 monthly revenue through organic, sustainable growth.

Named Young Entrepreneur of the Year 2024 in Espoo, Finland, Marianne built her own seven-figure company in her twenties entirely from scratch—with no audience, no connections, and no capital. Born and raised in a small town in Northern Finland by a single mother, and with a mixed cultural background, she understands deeply what it means to create opportunity out of nothing.

Marianne's journey from outsider to industry leader is living proof of what's possible with vision, resilience, and relentless execution. Her debut book, *Sivubisnes* (Otava, 2021), inspired a new wave of Nordic entrepreneurs to take bold steps toward their own dreams.

Driven by her mission to help one million women become too wealthy to be silenced, Marianne empowers women to own their power, speak their truth, and change the world through entrepreneurship. Looking ahead, her long-term vision is to become one of the most influential business voices of her generation—and to reshape the global conversation around leadership, wealth, and impact.

www.ingramcontent.com/pod-product-compliance
Lightning Source LLC
LaVergne TN
LVHW040141080526
838202LV00042B/2979